VIOLENCE AND UTOPIA

The Work of Jerome Boime

Edited by

Albert Boime

University Press of America, Inc.
Lanham • New York • London

Copyright © 1996 by
University Press of America,® Inc.
4720 Boston Way
Lanham, Maryland 20706

3 Henrietta Street
London, WC2E 8LU England

All rights reserved
Printed in the United States of America
British Cataloging in Publication Information Available

Library of Congress Cataloging-in-Publication Data

Boime, Jerome, 1934-1977.
Violence and Utopia : the work of Jerome Boime / edited by Albert Boime.
p. cm.
Includes index.
1. Boime, Jerome, 1934-1977. 2. Violence--United States. 3. Social conflict--United States. 4. Government, Resistance to--United States. 5. Marginality, Social--United States. I. Boime, Albert. II. Title.
HM281.858   1996   303.6'0973--dc20   96-12026 CIP

ISBN 0-7618-0323-8 (cloth: alk. ppr.)
ISBN 0-7618-0324-6 (pbk: alk. ppr.)

⊖™The paper used in this publication meets the minimum requirements of American National Standard for information Sciences—Permanence of Paper for Printed Library Materials, ANSI Z39.48—1984

FOR BENJAMIN

JERRY BOIME, M.A. 1960

Contents

Foreword v

Preface ix

Acknowledgments xiii

Brotherly Interlude I 1

The White Negro and the Northern Liberal 3

Brotherly Interlude II 7

A Political Interpretation Of Franz Kafka's The Trial 11

The Theater 49

Brotherly Interlude III 53

Does Political Discourse Have a Limit? 55

Brotherly Interlude IV 57

Violence and Myth: A Study of Georges Sorel 59

Brotherly Interlude V 79

Notes Towards an Understanding of Violence 81

Violence and Sociality 105

Allen Grossman's Poem "The Department" 123

Revision of Section II Violence and Myth:
   A Study of Georges Sorel 127

Second Revision Violence and Myth: A Study of Georges Sorel ... 133

Epilogue for my Brother 139

Index 156

FOREWORD

JERRY BOIME'S LONGING

Throughout the course of reading Jerry Boime's work, I felt strangely affected. It took me some time before I came upon some reasons for my shift from the evenness of everyday life to this agitation — heterogeneous reasons converging in my mood. One of them soon became obvious: the outrageous death of so gifted, groping, so longing a man, too young to have redeemed more than a small share of his large promise — in Allen Grossman's poem, fittingly included here, "[b]ereaved of mind by a weird truck." And I've been plagued by the failure of our department to obtain tenure for him, no matter how hard we tried: he had not published enough, thus could not stay at Brandeis, got a job in New Hampshire, and soon died, and I, as a member of the department, despite all good intentions and all efforts, am touched by a feeling of guilt. And there is yet another reason why I feel engaged by what Jerry wrote and by his fate: the pages that follow are not his alone but are a duet, sung by two brothers — a duet or a document, in which Jerry's part is the most important of all the reasons for my excitement since the core of Jerry's writing is in turn a document — of his groping and longing, which reflect his time and place.

I have to limit myself to the attempt at clarifying what I mean by the documentary character of Jerry's work. But first I must insist that this limitation does not imply that treating a text, or anything else, as a document produces an exhaustive assessment. On the contrary, it is only one of many approaches; above all, it must be distinguished from assessing

Violence and Utopia

something in respect to its validity (including its truth, logical cohesion, etc.). Thus I leave to others the question of the validity of Jerry's essays, particularly on Kafka's *The Trial* and on violence, the weightiest pieces of his writing.

The question that mobilizes Jerry to analyze *The Trial* is Kafka's question: what sense to make of Joseph K.'s arrest, "of this crucial, if painful experience ... a moment of startling clarity. ... The moment in its most critical aspect is lost, and this loss results in a most paradoxical turn of affairs. In order to make sense of the shock, we place it under systematic investigation. The ground rules for research procedures and subsequent theory construction involve a reduction ... to a common conceptual denominator (pp. 14-15)," which in Jerry's study of Kafka's novel is an analysis from a political perspective.

What is Jerry groping and longing for? The passage just quoted suggests that it is experience unmediated, unconceptualized, raw, which, however, if we would make sense of it, we must try to conceptualize or locate in a conceptualized structure. The quotation dates from 1960; a few years later, violence and, associated with it, fraternity, became his find on his search for immediacy. I don't think that what he says about them should be understood, any more than in Sorel himself, in a literal, everyday, empirical sense, but, precisely, as documenting this longing, as, in Sorel's terminology, "mythic." As Jerry shows:

> Mythic possession is ... an undivided state of heightened adoration, "free of reflection and all premeditated subtlety." The mythic image, e.g., Delacroix's "Liberty Leading the People," entirely fills the consciousness, and nothing else in the moment can exist apart from or beside itself. The ego presses all its energy on a single point, lives in it, loses itself in it (p. 69).

Ten years later, in 1974, Jerry contrasts this "mythic possession," this experience of complete absorption, with the consciousness that prevails in "civil life":

> Civil life provides a contingent means for the rational elaboration of mutual self-interest, but it cannot provide the basis for an ultimate assurance of unqualified association (p. 118).

Here the connection between complete absorption or "epic consciousness" and the idea of fraternity emerges. Fraternity, the outcome (or victim or precondition?) of violence, that is, deadly combat in which each of the (two) fighters risks his life, and "epic-consciousness" or undivided attention, are the two situations in which unmediated experience may occur. There must be reasons why Jerry comes upon these two, why he does not allow for such immediacy to be possible on innumerable other occasions, e. g., love, reading (whatever it may be, including Jerry's essays), seeing a cloud, confronting a problem (of whatever kind).

Jerry's admiration for fraternity and violence, the tragic end of his

Foreword

search, points to an awful danger, but he was perhaps too fulfilled by this admiration to alert us to it. The danger is that what he writes on violence and fraternity be taken literally, empirically, for if it were, it would affirm and proclaim the "vivere pericoloso" of fascism or, in its American version, "paramilitary culture." While Jerry must have been aware of this, he did not mention it possibly because he took it for granted that his ideas would be understood as documents of his groping and longing, thus of his time and place — which are ours still, and Kafka's and Sorel's as well.

Kurt H. Wolff
1994

Preface

Jerome Boime (1934-1977) began to seriously study the subject of violence in the early 1960s at the start of a decade just emerging from the repressive McCarthy era. As a student at the University of Chicago, he witnessed at first-hand the explosive conditions of the neighboring ghettoes. His reading of Franz Kafka's *The Trial* heightened his awareness of the State's capacity to victimize its citizenry for political purposes. In a sense Kafka's novel mediated between his self-awareness as a Jew in the aftermath of the Holocaust, and the contemporary local conditions created by the oppressive social system. It is no coincidence that his two articles in the University of Chicago's magazine *Phoenix* of 1961 include a macabre Kafkaesque story of exclusion and appropriation and duplicity and an interview addressing the issue of the manipulation of black people by Northern liberals.

Kafka was very much in Jerry's mind in this period and formed the subject of his Master's thesis, submitted in 1960. There he was concerned with the interpretation of the novel from "the standpoint of the citizen in an encounter with political authority." While it carries many standard academic obligations in the way of explanation and disclaimer, it nevertheless is a striking example of his analytic power and challenges the discipline of political science through an exploration of a medium marginal to the sector of traditional competence. It is a cogent study of the psychology of the novel and its capacity to inform political thought. His concern with social relations in the context of state authority anticipates his involvement with the dynamic of the fraternal order in his most mature work.

Violence and Utopia

After Kafka the most important influence on Jerry's thought was Georges Sorel. We spent part of the summers of 1962 and 1964 together at the *Bibliothèque Nationale*, Paris systematically going through the publications of Sorel, and we made so much racket that readers around us kept hushing us up. Sorel's writings were the subject of his PhD proposal and his incisive and original critique paved the way for his own theoretical understanding of social violence. Jerry formulated his proposal for his mentor Hannah Arendt (who described it as "excellent") the year Kennedy was assassinated, and developed it in fuller detail the year of the Gulf of Tonkin resolution. The conditions in which his thought unfolded now exploded into the violence of Vietnam and domestic upheaval. The simultaneous occurrence of war abroad and civil war at home set the perimeters for Jerry's research. His analysis of classical studies of violence was energized every day by actual events. In this way theory and fact complemented one another. He saw exemplified in the clash of students with police over University policy — in the Civil Rights struggle, the very theories he was working out in the scholarly domain. It was like a 'pure' mathematician developing a set of equations with instant applications to the real world. Political assassinations, urban and campus revolts, military violence, and the emergence of a technology-dependent terrorism inevitably kept his attention focused on a theoretical explanation and the need for a theoretical solution.

Following my brother's papers, I will attempt to summarize his views with the help of his notes, the contributions of his students, friends and colleagues, and the memory of our conversations. It is of course proverbial to state that group solidarity requires enemies. The threat that issues from without generates the incentives for societies to surmount their ordinary divisions and unite against the common enemy. The construction of an adversary as savage and depraved also constitutes an ideological strategy for bolstering the traditional values and customs of one's own community. The difference of the opponent helps reinforce the norms of the members of the antagonistic group. An unfortunate consequence of this social logic is that absent an external menace a society may designate groups or individuals within its own body to function as surrogates for the foreign foe. Such "homemade" deviants become indispensable to societies in times of crisis when fundamental values are being challenged: the persecution of the projected nemesis then serves to reaffirm the dominant group's norms and ideological presuppositions.

It was Jerry, however, who demonstrated the dynamics of this process with his discovery of "the fraternal order." He methodically analyzed the systems of political exclusion which enabled him to spell out the process of bonding that occurs in the ritual persecution of one's enemies and the ritual affirmation of the communal norms. In this country, we have witnessed vivid examples in the personality cults of Jim Jones, Bhagwan Shree Rajneesh, and David Koresh. The massacre of the Branch Davidians

Preface

in Waco, Texas, organized and abetted by the state, is only the latest case of an ongoing phenomenon. It is to my brother's everlasting credit that his analysis can help us understand the global dynamics of the Holocaust in Europe as well as the local dynamics of the holocaust at Mt. Carmel. He would have been struck, I am sure, by the coincidence of the Waco tragedy falling on the fiftieth anniversary of the Nazi assault on the Jewish ghetto in Warsaw, Poland.

As every theoretician of violence and student of animal behavior knows, human beings are unique in their tendency to intraspecific murder and in their self-consciousness. While animals fight and occasionally kill intraspecifically, most often one of the antagonists retreats. Predators engage their victims for survival, never for removing them as a threat to their survival. Human beings alone fight to the death and systematically massacre members of their own species: holocaust and genocide are uniquely human terms. We have succeeded so effectively in discovering ways of eliminating each other that we have reached a point where the entire human race could be destroyed in a matter of minutes. Other species have become extinct because the environment changed too rapidly for the species to adjust. The human situation is the reverse. Instead of being overtaken by the environment, human beings have overtaken the environment they now menace so entirely. The environment has been altered at the price of the animal. The human ancestors' capacity to change the environment may well have proved to be our undoing. I will return to that point in the Epilogue For My Brother.

Albert Boime
1994

Acknowledgments

All previous published statements of my debts to others must pale in comparison to this one, since the measure of support in the present instance often went way beyond intellectual guidance, information, and instruction to include emotional and nurturing sustenance during many years of the grieving process. Thus I am expressing here more than mere gratitude and appreciation for individual contributions to the realization of the enterprise, but also the awareness that my survival in the world depended upon their generous and loving attachment to Jerry and me and this project.

First of all, I want to embrace my immediate family, Myra, Robert and Eric whose love and sympathetic insight sustained me especially during the trying period of research when poring over Jerry's handwritten notes and papers placed such an enormous strain on my emotional life. My sister, Ruth Kohn, my brother and sister-in-law, Irv and Melody Boime, were also always strongly supportive and understanding. My debt to my sister-in-law, Dorothy Boime, is equally profound for her unhesitating encouragement, her generosity in making available so much of the documentation, and for sharing with me her vivid personal insights and memories. The searching questions and interest of my nephew Benjamin Boime kept me on track and helped me more than he might have realized.

Jerry's close friend, Charles Levy, was always available during the painful early days, and his memories, perceptive grasp of events, and psychological clarity also constituted part of my healing process. In addition, Charlie provided me with the precious cartons of Jerry's notes which were stored in his basement — henceforth to be known as the "Jerry Boime Archives."

Jerry's dear friends David and Rosy Abelson and Janet and Sam Rosenkrantz also provided me with valuable documentation and early eye-witness testimony, and, above all, kept me going by sharing with me the warm and enduring remembrances of their relationship with Jerry as well as helping to clarify for me the wellsprings of his contributions.

I want to also express my gratitude to Jerry's colleagues at Brandeis, Irving Zola, Maurice Stein, Allen Grossman, Egon Bittner, and Kurt Wolff. Irving Zola made available to me valuable departmental documents and Maurice Stein's encouragement at a critical moment helped strengthen me in my determination to publish the project. Allen Grossman, whose stirring, compassionate, and unsettling poem on Jerry has been cathartic for me during my periodic bouts with depression when remembering, also fortified my efforts to realize the publication of Jerry's "big Thought." Egon Bittner and Kurt Wolff graciously consented to read the manuscript and made suggestions for changes and improvements that were indispensable to me. I am especially grateful to Professor Wolff for his foreword that is a moving tribute to Jerry's intellectual "longing."

Finally, my greatest personal and professional debt is to my perceptive fellow art historian, Wayne Andersen, who practically took charge of the manuscript in a period when I was despairing at ever seeing it through to realization. He understood, to use his own words, "that a surgeon cannot operate on someone he loves." A multi-talented personality who would have been at home in Renaissance Florence, Wayne not only took precious time out of his own hectic schedule to give the manuscript a close and sympathetic reading, he also helped me to rearrange it and format it professionally on his computer. The finished product he returned exalted me to the point of feeling that at last I could serve my brother's memory with a fair measure of justice. For this I owe him more than can ever be easily articulated in the formal ritual of "acknowledgments."

BROTHERLY INTERLUDE I

When Malcolm X spoke at the University of Chicago in the fall of 1961, he held up to the audience a copy of the school's magazine, the *Phoenix*, and called attention to an interview in its pages on black-white relations. He praised the comments of the interviewee for what he considered to be their accurate insight into the current tense situation. Considering that in 1961 the civil rights movement had yet to find its momentum and Malcolm X's eloquent voice had yet to be heard above the modest call for ending segregation, Jerry's interview is an astonishing document resonating with the thought of the fiery advocate of black liberation and separatism.

In formulating a coherent explanation of the black's struggle against internalized white racism, Jerry's all-too-brief interview also represents a crucial stage in his own thinking about the problem of violence in American society. As Jerry glimpsed earlier than most scholars of his generation, the "Negro" was and remains a social construct of white people to fulfill their own economic and emotional needs. Treated as subhuman and invested with only the rights of a beast, black peoples' humanity was suppressed and their physical being appropriated to pave the way for and contribute to the development of American capitalism. Malcolm X turned the strategy on itself, preaching separatism and black nationalism against the doctrine of white supremacy.

Jerry's brief interview touched on themes that would become central to Malcolm X's ideological position: the issue of the construction of social identity, the integrationists' encouragement of the rise of a black bourgeoisie whose interests were inimical to the masses — what the Black Muslim leader called "twentieth-century House Negroes" — and the deceptive siren call of the Northern liberals who perpetuated the myth that freedom could be found north of the Mason-Dixon Line. Both

Malcolm X and Jerry pointed to the inherent contradictions of black-white relations which is constituted by white domination. Using the metaphor of masks (perhaps derived from Frantz Fanon whose *Black Skin, White Masks* had not yet been published in English), Jerry enunciated the black sense of self as a negative image of the white and reduced to the vanishing point in civil life. On this view, the black became the quintessential Other of American life whose oppression served as the rallying point for white society.

Perhaps one of the most astonishing parallels between Malcolm X's thought and Jerry's interview is a passage in the *Autobiography*, where Malcolm recalls the Swerlins, surrogate white parents who ran a detention home:

> What I am trying to say is that it just never dawned on them that I could understand, that I wasn't a pet, but a human being. They didn't give me credit for having the same sensitivity, intellect and understanding that they would have been ready and willing to recognize in a white boy in my position ... Even though they appeared to have opened the door, it was still closed. Thus they never did see me.

And here is Jerry responding to a question, two years before Alex Haley began his series of interviews with Malcolm X:

> Take James Baldwin for an example. He responds by saying "Nobody Knows My Name." In other words, he is not recognized as a discrete entity — as James Baldwin — but rather as the inescapable abstraction. He is differentiated only by his color. But this relegates him to anonymity — an anonymous threat. He is no one man in particular because he is seen, for better or for worse, as every Negro in general, totally depersonalized. He belongs only to a dark, agitated herd, and outside of it he has no possibility. I leave it to you to imagine how this treatment affects a man like Baldwin, a man of remarkable sensitivity and acute self-consciousness. Such a man can only end up despising his own color and hating those who enforce this fixed identity upon him.

Finally, Jerry's reference to Baldwin attests to his own personal need to remove exclusionary boundaries and to hear the voice of the never-heard and the never-seen, and this is no token gesture since throughout the interview he quotes from blacks to clarify his explanations. He does not speak for blacks as a representative of an academic institution, but takes his discourse out into the street. Jerry's sharp understanding of the great divide between black and white, and of the alternative versions proposed by adversaries and opponents surely played a role in his formulation of "the fraternal order." Thus he readied himself to interpret the urban insurrections, religious and cultural nationalism, and student movements looming upon the horizon.

THE WHITE NEGRO AND THE NORTHERN LIBERAL

(1961)

An Interview with Jerome Boime
Phoenix, Fall 1961, pp. 15-16.

Interviewer: Norman Mailer's "The White Negro" suggests that the northern Negro has two strategies; to live in humiliation or to live drugged and dangerously.

JB: Well, let me put it most directly. Mailer's standpoint assumes the bestiality of the Negro and his culture. To be sure this beast is romantic, but he is nonetheless "On his fours." The "white Negro" is an extraordinary articulation of common, if unadmitted attitudes, that are deeply felt in the North. The animalization of the minority is not suspended beyond the Mason Dixon line; it is curiously inverted. The "black beast of the racist South is transformed into "man's best friend" in the liberal North. The mark of oppression becomes an apotheosis. If the Negro is degraded in the South because he is treated as a special kind of animal, he is deified in the North because he is treated as a special kind of animal. But the fundamental misapprehension is shared. The liberal and the racist only fall out over the question of the "dignity" of the "beast". This question was given classical expression in Charles Carrol's bizarre book, "The Negro: Beast or the image of God?" published over sixty years ago.

I: Mailer's title is no less arresting and no less revealing. Why?

JB: Well, the white man becomes his favorite animal. Shocking? Consider Kafka's "Metamorphosis." If a man can become a roach certainly he can become a Negro. Here is the hipster's thrill and the liberal's ideology combined: they become Negroes for a night.... "Those people see the world differently than we do, living in the eternal present as they do. If only we could get into their wild shoes...." Here you discover the mystique of the "dangerous Negro" and one is almost tempted to say, a pornographic interest in the exotic life of the forbidden animal. What makes him tick, you know, what is at the heart of his darkness.

I: How does the Negro respond to this not so subtle treatment?

JB: Take James Baldwin for an example. He responds by saying "Nobody Knows My Name." In other words, he is not recognized as a discrete identity — as James Baldwin — but rather as the inescapable abstraction. He is differentiated only by his color. But this relegates him to anonymity — an anonymous threat. He is no one man in particular because he is seen, for better or for worse, as every Negro in general, totally depersonalized. He belongs only to a dark, agitated herd, and outside of it he has no possibility. I leave it to you to imagine how this treatment affects a man like Baldwin, a man of remarkable sensitivity and acute self-consciousness. Such a man can only end up despising his own color and hating those who enforce this fixed identity upon him.

I should say, by the way, that this term "treatment" is quite appropriate, for the Negro is manipulated even by people with the best intentions. As one Negro put it to me, "I always feel I'm on some white man's banner." Thus in New York, Chicago, Detroit, the Negro is kept in his place. To be sure, the meaning of keeping the Negro in his place is quite different in the South. The quarantine of the northern Negro is rather a "splendid" isolation, an isolation that produces a rhythmic genius, an ecstatic vocabulary, and an unceasing quest for risks.

Well, let's take the most sophisticated and progressive environment, the University neighborhood, and consider the relationships. Is the line actually crossed? You must ask yourself: what is the spontaneous reaction? What feelings are released when the Negro enters the white man's space? You get what we might call a double take. The initial reaction approximates: "Here comes the dark man out of the untamed depths. What is he doing in our world?" The pigmentation of skin is after all no less a desperate possession than a car or a suit of clothes. The difference is that you can sell the car and take off the suit. But almost immediately this reaction is counteracted by another: "What has color got to do with it? A Negro is as good as anyone else, maybe in his own way — better." We've got a real struggle here, high tension, and this tension may explain the striking theatrics of the Negro-white encounter. It is theatrical because powerful feelings are released and then held back. These feelings are difficult to manage even by the most cultivated. The performance is bound to be grotesque. The exaggerated camaraderie, the unrelenting sympathy for the Negro's misfortune, the lyrical celebration of the Negro folk culture, the inflated promises, the "we're all in this together" business, all this bewilders the colored man because he is not certain as to what this "together" involves. What is most paradoxical in all these expressions of love is the conspicuous absence of intimacy. He is loved by definition, not by virtue of any personal attachment. He is the white man's brother even before he is introduced. This earnest performance rarely convinces the Negro even when he plays along. Not to play along can only embarrass. A Negro student put it this way: "When white boys get together they talk about girls. When a white boy meets a Negro, he talks about brotherhood." The Negro is painfully sensitized to the double take, especially if he has grown up in an interracial neighborhood. The Negro has seen the mask slip all too often. He asks, "Where do these people go when the neighborhood is tipped, the racial balance upset? What happens to all that 'brotherhood'?" Well, easy come, easy go. The embarrassing condition of the interracial neighborhood is that one of the two races in it always prepared to leave. You see, the color line is not overcome by coexistence.

I: You say the Negro "plays along" in this "drama." Could you explain?

JB: Well, the Negro, once given the opportunity, strives to escape his stigmatized identity, more specifically those attributes which the white world animalizes. So you find the Negro middle class, the "black bourgeoisie," in panic. This panic is all too obvious. You hear it in the conspicuous cultivation of the anglicized accent, you see it in the practiced elegance. Take the Negro lawyer who says candidly that he "wouldn't dare eat watermelon." The Negro in this example becomes a caricature of the middle class. Having arrived, he tends to isolate and disdain those Negroes at the bottom who cannot or will not move upward into the collective "fadeout," into the white middle class. Now you've got two professional human beings on your hands: the white Negro and the "fading" Negro. And when these two meet, you have a real show, for each reinforces the deception of the other until they are literally abstracted out of existence. This is tragicomedy, you see, because both actors have a futile wish to trade roles. The Negro tries to "pass" and the white man "slums". This recalls the ironic insight of the Baptist preacher: "I don't understand what all this racial tension is about. After all, the white folks keep going to Florida to get black, and the Negroes keep putting on the face cream to get white. So we ought to blend real nice." The point is, of course, that the white man's not for blending. So this pretense of interchangeability fools no one. The cosmetic cannot completely conceal the face or the feelings.

I: You speak of the "fadeout" of the Negro. Is this artificial equality of the Negro middle class the way of the future?

JB: Now you raise a naughty question which is better kept underground. But let's take a chance and discuss it openly. Your question, you know, implies that the Negro is playing a losing game, even as his civil rights and economic opportunities expand. The Negro community is not unaware of the dilemma. What is the price of Negro freedom? Transformation into the distorted shadow of the white middle class. This is no mean toll to pay to get through the social turnstile. The immigrant, the "hyphenated American", has this problem too, but he is not visibly out of place in any newly acquired status. The social bases of the Negro's civil rights are precarious. They are "shadow" rights.

The white liberal is also caught up in this dilemma. On the one hand he wants to maintain the rhythm, the spontaneity, of the Negro folk culture. On the other hand he wants to draw the Negro into the "respectable" merry-go-round of the white middle class. But you can't have it both ways. The one choice is made at the expense of the other. But the liberal refuses to recognize this dilemma, because he wants "his" Negro to be both a "unique beast" and an equal shadow". Indeed this ambivalence might very well define the crisis of northern liberalism.

Brotherly Interlude II

Jerry's interview included a reference to Kafka's *Metamorphosis* — the tale of a human being reduced to the plane of an insect. For Jerry to have been so engrossed in Kafka's writings in that period was surely rare in academia, although since that time the burgeoning body of secondary literature devoted to Kafka attests to his profound appeal to the modern imagination. This is not the place to rehearse the history of Kafka's reception since his death in 1924, but it is a history that encompasses such stalwart names as Walter Benjamin, Theodor Adorno, Albert Camus, Jean-Paul Sartre, and, more recently, Harold Bloom and Jacques Derrida. Recent studies systematically seek to challenge the stereotyped image of Kafka as the isolated, alienated author who spun out allegories on the isolation and alienation of the individual, but as far back as 1961 Jerry tried to break through this conventional screen of understanding. Not least of all, Jerry plucked from Kafka's writing some of the crucial issues that later scholars would seize upon including the elimination of specific cultural signs that had traditionally served to situate a literary text in time and space, the suspension of material laws and social norms that hinted at the author's moral reference, and even the seeming disappearance of the author from his own text — a phenomenon that Jerry satirically allegorizes in his short parable, *The Theater*, that here follows the essay on *The Trial*.

Jerry's profound meditation on *The Trial* set the stage for his subsequent investigation of the sociology of violence. Joseph K. is excluded from the community for an unspecified crime, thus denying him the possibility of raising his juridical voice. He is the designated subhuman for driving the state's ideological apparatus. Although actual events transformed the story of Joseph K. into a prophetic anticipation of the fate awaiting European Jews in World War II, Jerry resisted looking at the work either as an allegorical portent of National Socialism and the Holocaust or as a key to unraveling Kafka's mental life or biography. Instead, he dealt with the *Trial* as a self-contained text with its own internal structure. His aim was to show the potential of a novel to inform the study of politics, at the same time revealing the limitations of the methods and organization of the discipline of political science itself. If K.'s experience could be seen to resemble the form of theories of instrumental terror conjured up by political scientists, or the traditional argument of scapegoating needed to divert public attention from real political and economic problems, these insights were still inadequate to explain Auschwitz. Jerry's analysis of Kafka's novel supplies the dynamic that mapped the progressive degradation of a person before extermination. K. is trapped from the start in a position of utter helplessness before being delivered into the clutches of the state. Long familiar to students of structuralism and deconstruction, this concentration on the text independent of the author's biography was a unique approach and certainly out of synch with the prevailing methods and content of political science at the time of its writing. Nor did Jerry fetishize the work as a "timeless" or canonical creation that transcended everyday life. Instead, he showed how the structure of Kafka's fiction retained and amplified the initiating conditions governing all exploratory research — that point of origin that tends to get suppressed in the more formalized aspects of academic scholarship.

A brief word on Jerry's short piece entitled *The Theater*. The protagonist of this parable is a theater impresario who tells the audience that the evening's performance has been canceled. Kafka made much use of theatrical themes and the figure of the impresario in such writings as "In the Penal Colony," "A Hunger Artist," and Josephine the Singer." Kafka himself became an impresario for a time for the traveling Yiddish theater of Yitzhak Löwy, and spoke publicly in his role as impresario at Löwy's final performance in Prague. In his writings, however, It would seem that the theater operated as metaphor for the nightmarish world under faceless bureaucratic management.

Jerry's first-person impresario-narrator presides in the form of existential crisis control manager, first announcing the cancellation of the evening performance and then keeping the audience orderly. But gradually we come to see that the crisis is in the thinking of the impresario alone, who splits into the multiple entities of audience and acting troupe, and by the tale's end nothing is certain any longer, neither the impresario's self nor the external reality in which he supposedly functions. I believe that Jerry's *Theater* serves as a gloss for his study of *The Trial*, in which the customary views of reality within the closed container of society are reversed and formulated into startling paradoxes. The narrative increasingly takes a subversive turn that makes visible the arbitrariness of its very structure, thus undermining it in the process of its unfoldment.

As in *The Trial*, all phenomena appear as masks or made-up faces that have to be stripped away to reveal the true look of things. In the end, the impresario-narrator calls his own existence into question, talking himself out of a job, just as Jerry did in his position as professor at Brandeis. The brilliant performance of self-effacement is Jerry's strategy for showing the arbitrary rules of academic exposition that all too often serves as the rationale for bureaucratic actions in the real world.

A Political Interpretation Of Franz Kafka's *The Trial*

(1960)

Franz Kafka's stories invite a multitude of interpretations ranging from nonhesitant imputations of psychoanalysis to the concoctions of the esoteric cabal. But the variety of standpoints in no way mitigates the dogma of the individual schools of thought. Each claims to deliver authoritative meaning from Kafka's work while dismissing claims of competitors for the "sacred" platform.

The presumption of "final" explanations ironically conflicts with the author's modest intentions. Kafka did not wish his "little allegory" to be understood under strict formula. He ruled out an exclusive exegesis. He can only complete three fourths of the puzzle; the final quarter is impossible to complete. Not because there are too few pieces but too many. The linking chains of human experience cannot be resolved on one note. The final passage is a riot of alternatives. This voice speaks in radical contrast to its interpretive listeners. The many attempts to foreclose Kafka's meaning have produced a comic competition of symbolism trekking to a rhetorical impasse: Who's got the right symbol?[1] Kafka would have been confounded by this question. He did not presume to resolve the meaning of his pieces once and for all. Final resolution excludes the refracted gleaming, the absent minded 'wandering off' that carries the compelling "off-stage" insight. We cannot afford to refuse the unsuspected silences and enlightening distractions that break through *our* schedule of expectations. Truth lurks behind doors we dare not open — we should not continually use the one most opened. There is a goal but no one way to it; what we call "the way" is only tentative. One must be faithful to the options, to the indetermination and ambiguity of human events. As Walter Kaufman observed, "Ambiguity is the essence of his art,"[2] which means, for Kafka, that the essence of life is its generosity of interpretations. But Kafka is not an obscurantist; his is the ambiguity that forces reconsideration of those facile, truth-defying categories that for comfort's sake we are prone to establish. A fence is not needed but a platform. Kafka writes to explore — not confine, not suggest, not resolve.

On this understanding of Kafka, we submit the political interpretation of his great work, *The Trial*. This interpretation is presented as only one among many alternative approaches. We do not claim to resolve *The Trial* on this single explanation, but take this novel as a cue to a mode of suggestive analysis; i.e., the standpoint of the citizen in an encounter with political authority.

The Trial, on this view can be seen as a political novel, or, if you will, a political allegory because its central event is the arbitrary arrest and execution of an "innocent" (unwitting) man. Kafka provided us with a modest confidence when he wrote in his notebooks, "The extraordinary impact of politics is only realized when we forget ourselves, our private stations. I am now describing a man (Joseph K.) who takes this realization only after he has lost himself."[3] Unfortunately, we cannot resuscitate Kafka for further testimony and we cannot be certain that the political interpretation of the novel coincides with Kafka's plan, if indeed he had a "plan." In any respect, *The Trial* lends itself to many points of view because it is a "platform" and not a "fence." We therefore feel justified in taking Kafka's suggestion and developing an interpretation around the striking political implications of this book. It is not meant to challenge or exclude other interpretations but rather to complement them. In the end, all interpretations are disarmed of their presumption by the artist himself. "The myth tries to explain the unexplainable. As it comes out of the ground of truth, it must end again in the unexplainable."[4]

Contribution of the Novel to the Study of Politics

The contribution of a novel neither emanates from the organized body of inventoried research nor issues out of exclusive channels devoted to professional controversy among political scientists. Literary insight into matters political is off the "beaten track", is thus deprived of the legitimacy that only discipline can confer. Nonetheless, it is here suggested that the indirect approach of literature to the political sector can open up unexpected rewards. We will show that the independence and distance of the literary medium from methods and organization of political science is the basis of a unique contribution to meaningful literature.

G. E. Moore remarked: "When we refine our impressions to obtain a graduating synthesis; when we bundle up discrete events to achieve the satisfaction of a massive explanation; we have made a definite progress; but we also have left something behind; we have 'systematically' forgotten our initial incentive and have to be reminded of our motivating problem."[5] Correspondingly, the thought process involved in the study of politics is initially activated by distinct, temporally grounded disturbances of our routine perceptions; but when we pass on to analysis, we are transcending our first-hand contact with the newly disturbed environment and systematically forgetting the motivation that impelled us to investigate in the first place. The impact of a decisive political event generates, for a variety of reasons, a succeeding inquiry, but in this irreversible move to inquiry the event is pinched out of the vital context; it dies as it stings.

At the moment the significant event occurs it gains our spontaneous attention. We cannot view any other development of greater moment and we consequently give it an intense and undivided concern. This rapt concentration suggests that we are profoundly involved in the "eventful" situation and are compelled, for the time being, to exclude other perceptions that are not immediately relevant to it; but when the event has given way in time, when it is no longer new to us, we are content with the residual products of "second thought" and attend to it only as "one among the many" projects of research. We process the event after we have, so to speak, taken our eyes off it. "As already baptized into the life of the mind it (the event) moves on to the plane of universality."[6]

Because the unique intersection of conditions producing this disturbance no longer applies, the disturbance is no longer taken as first perceived. Accordingly, we cannot reply to the event as we did when we were in the position to receive it as a first experience. As a result of this irretrievable loss of presence, we are left with the alternative of reducing the precise moment and the discrete location of the incident to a "fitted" historic position where it is no longer viewed for itself alone. Droysen, the German historian, noted that when we look back at "historic" occasions, we view them in a quite different way from that in which they occurred, and which they had in the wishes and deeds of those who enacted them. So it is not a paradox to ask how History (*Geschichte*) comes out of transactions (*Geschaeften*), and what, with this transfer into another medium, as it were, is added or lost.[7]

When we view the event as history, we have already relaxed the distinct hold this event had on us when it initially intervened in our regime of expectations; the event now receives importance only insofar as it joins the homogeneous strength of its class of historical associates. We have in a profound respect broken our direct tie with the event; a tie that when first engaged was unequivocal and compelling. Hannah Arendt, for example, suggests this difficulty in confronting recent political developments: "We can escape from its [totalitarianism] impact only if we decide not to focus our attention on its very nature, but let it run away into the interminable connections and similarities which certain tenets of totalitarian doctrine necessarily show with familiar theories of occidental thought."[8]

But it is difficult to sustain our unwavering stare of the event that first captured our attention. It is far from comforting to keep our eyes in unrelieved focus on the image of an annihilated Lidice — it is much easier to attempt an escape from the extraordinary impact of this event. Indeed it would be quite unfortunate if we could not shift our attention from the point of severe stress, and buffer ourselves from the initial disturbance by resuming the routine and moderate pattern that preceded the disturbance, or by readjusting to the post-crisis situation by the installation of a more sophisticated set of consolatory responses. Shock is momentary in the aforementioned cases, but if the state of shock continues for a protracted duration, we speak of mental collapse.

The resurgence of the personality depends upon a brief stay of the radical distress and upon disabusing the overweighted expectations which gave rise to that distress. Yet as we successfully pass on from the painful moment we are concurrently covering the traces of the most decisive expression of the human temperament. For what is most fundamental to the personality is revealed by the reactions ensuing from the transitory psychic disturbance. The sudden appearance of the unexpected in the network of our day-to-day arrangements precipitates all at once a severe eruption of beliefs and aspirations. Indeed, we can know a man by what shocks him. More is clear in the single moment of anticipated (and hence unmitigated) exposure than in a lifetime of unchallenged and unexamined moral pretensions. In a shattering instant of recognition the whole superstructure of precarious conventions and expectations are given the lie — and fall.

When we say that shock represents a break with our past and a collapse of our illusory hopes, we are also saying that it marks the onset of a reorientation to the fresh situation which is created by our radical disillusionment. We purportedly carry on in spite of the pivotal upset, but "this carrying on in spite of" is a turn toward a new dimension. We disengage the bewildering experience from its unendurable context and employ secondary modes of explanation to cover our retreat from it. This retreat is supported by the failure of the memory to depict faithfully an event of profound emotional significance. The inexorable passage of time can only accentuate the distance we put between our mind and the "loaded" incident. This distance, in turn, allows us an expansive freedom of interpretation as the event grows ever more remote in time, and hence less susceptible to check and surveillance. Thus the dissolution of this crucial, if painful, experience serves to blur and anesthetize a moment of startling clarity — a moment which places before us and reduces to a point of focal release the elaborate system of beliefs. It is a rare election to disastrous enlightenment.

The moment in its most critical aspect is lost, and this loss results in a most paradoxical turn of affairs. In order to make sense of the shock, we place it under systematic investigation. The ground rules for research procedure and subsequent theory construction involve a reduction of the multitudinous nuclear events to a common conceptual denominator.

The minimum requirement that the political theorist demands of a datum admissible to his formulation is its interchangeability in some way with another datum. This reduction of events is the prerequisite for their admission to his formulation. Only as these events are "cut to size" to fit the uniform specifications of a fixed historical chronology, do they achieve the symmetrical relation necessary for their comparison and contrast. Thus, in order to deal with these events on the level of analysis, it is indispensable that they be commensurable by a common standard, i.e., the historical field. The function of history is akin in this respect to the function of the monetary market where accepted currency is exchanged in specific denominations. The political analyst (like the capital speculator) manipulates the currency of the common market of history to obtain sufficient credit to support his long-term investment, i.e., his philosophic position.

Thus in the attempt to understand political events it is necessary to convert them into "negotiable" units. Without this denominational conversion the task of isolating comparative causal linkages could not be carried on. This breaking down of these irreversible events into convertible units allows historical events to play the mirror for each other — even if the reflection is cast from a distance of three thousand years. In this manner the attempt is made to duplicate or "homogenize" for the purposes of theoretical uniformity, temporarily distinct circumstances.[9]

History viewed as the homogeneous reserve of convertible units, presupposes equality, or parity of events. The attempt to level and denominate the rush of time into manageable history is understandable because the novelty and heterogeneity of experiential time is altogether antithetical to the uniform requirements of historical analysis. Thus this erasure of time is necessary to the very survival of a systematic investigation of politics. F. H. Bradley speaks of the temporal loss in a related context. The whole movement of our mind implies the disregard of time. Not only does intellect accept what is true once for what is true always but the whole mass of what is called 'association' implies the same principle. The associated elements are divorced from their temporal context and are set free in union and ready to form fresh union without regard for time's reality. This is in effect to degrade time to the level of appearance.

In the act of degrading time we are trying to get behind the ephemeral presentations that bow successively before our view. In the attempt to sustain our hold over the disintegrating components of our past that are no longer available to our immediate environment, we are forced to bridle the unrestricted proliferation of time by translating these escaping temporal positions into a series of fixed points, cross-related on a plotted historical field.

This intractable quest for uniformity, fixity, and timelessness in history often disposes the political historian to overlook the incomparable and irreversible aspects of distinct historical situations. To be sure, he feels that the peculiarities of the fading event is faithfully revived in the form of a manageable representation that "stands for" the irreparable loss of actual presence. But the representation cannot make up for the loss even though it may give us the deceptive confidence that we have lost nothing. The event, in spite of the presumption, cannot "stand before us" in the abstract.

The set of massive characteristics which significant political events hold in common certainly must be accounted for, but there is an upper limit to the scope of this accounting procedure. One of these limits or negative effects is the attenuation of the peculiar temporal impression of a political event for the sake of establishing analytic uniformity. Political analysis incurs an unavoidable liability by the very nature of its investment. The loss is entailed in the foundation of the discipline — the sacrifice is time.

We are led to ask: Is there a medium outside the sector of competence of traditional political science which might complement the loss it suffers by allowing a simulated re-entry into the duration of significant political events that have been transformed into "history"?

Goethe perceived a certain virtue in preserving our critical early experiences as they evolve in psychological time because, as he expressed it, "the satisfied man is one who can see the connection between the end and the beginning of his life." But how is it possible to recapture or vivify the image of the beginning (the motivating incidents) as these images were presented in the beginning? How can we regain the irretrievable past and reverse the irreversible? How can we turn topsy-turvy the unidirectional causal order and unscramble the eggs?

It is certain that we cannot break the physical bounds of our position in the present, but can we not take leave of our "base of reality" by entering into an independent, albeit fictitious time sequence? Now this trick the self plays on its immediate environment can only be executed by the subject taking the place, so to speak, of another in time. We endure in time only as distinct human individuals and we can take leave of our ongoing identity only by entering the independent duration of another individual. We thus get out of our time only by getting into the shoes of someone else. Proust noticed this transformation when he wrote, " a single minute released from the chronological order of time has recreated in us a human being similarly released."[11]

The genius of the literary creation inheres precisely in this capacity to attract us into the shoes of a constructed individual in evolution. The novel, particularly, has the task of tempting the reader to assume the role of the character appearing on page one and maintaining us in the station of that assumed character until the novel ends, i.e., finishes with the characterization of the individual. "A second ago we were in Parma with Count Mosca and La Sanseverina, with Clelia and Fabrice; we lived their lives with them, immersed in their atmosphere, their time and place."[12] We are ushered out from our standing identity and transported to the temporal-spatial world of one who is undergoing an experience that is significant and compelling enough that we should wish to enter into it. Ibsen, for one, emphasized the importance of intercepting his audience's vision. "My object was to make the reader feel he was going through a piece of real experience."[13] Paul Valéry asks us to imagine ourselves in a state of transport from a work of art, one of those works which compel us to desire them all the more, the more we possess them the more they possess us. We feel the work acting upon us suits us so well that we cannot imagine it as different. In certain cases of supreme satisfaction we even feel that we are being transformed in some profound way, becoming someone whose sensibility is capable of such fullness of delight and immediate comprehension.[14]

In the process of reading through the novel we are reproducing the moment of the literary character in our self. We thus overcome our environing present only by taking possession of or being "possessed" by the development of a Sorel, a Karamazov, an Ilyitch or a Rubashov. In so doing we receive their history as our own. It is in this projected dimension that the present takes on breadth of its own and allows us, as William James remarked, "to look from two directions into time."[15]

If we can be induced to take this position in a fictitious time-slice with a character or set of characters sympathetic to our own disposition,[16] we can by association elaborate our own beliefs through them. We test and reveal our otherwise untested and unrevealed assumptions by proxy. We are forced to admit these assumptions as we are carried through the ongoing development of the literary characterization. By identifying with the problems of the depicted individual we are ushered into an arena of shifting alternatives and are called upon to make judgment. We have to decide because we cannot stay the intercepting demands of the situation we accept, for the time being, as our own. If we do not resolve our attitude in the moment the event appears before us, we have forfeited the advantage of clarifying our own sentiments. Then we are altering the quality of our accepted values, suspending the commitments they make on us, when we remove them from this point of contact in time. This abandonment of spontaneous judgment is not a consequence of regained composure or of cooling down of our "hot blood" in light of sober reflection. On the contrary, we still maintain, after considerable re-examination, our first conviction and are furthermore persuaded of the legitimacy of our initial response, e.g., our repugnance at genocide. The peculiar difficulty inheres in the failure of our convictions, already accepted as legitimate, to move us as they did when they were first made manifest. When our values are carried in the abstract we relinquish what is absolutely essential to them, namely, their timeliness. We are cut off from the provocative conditions that activated our cluster of attachments. We do not undergo our value-trial as we first endured it.

The mediation of the masterwork of literature, on the other hand, involves us in the phases of expression of the individual personality and draws us into the dynamic evolution of a moral crisis. We unwittingly release our own sentiments when we accept — by our persistence in the reading — the world of the novel as an arena for our own actions. The advantage of this vicarious value test is profound because we are but rarely subjected to a critical trial in our own life. These moments, otherwise inaccessible to us, can be reproduced in the temporal art of literature. Thomas Mann observed that "time is the medium of narration as it is the medium of life."[17]

To the extent that the political novel reproduced in the reader a correlative response involving a deep attachment to the fictional environment, the reader comes to define himself on a critical issue. The student of politics cannot be unconcerned with the crucial initiating experiences that inspire his research. The political novel allows us to reconfront one of these initiating experiences as it unfolds before an individual undergoing an encounter with political authority. The medium of literature can present these experiences in their distinct duration as a cue to the recall of the origin of our removed analysis.

These pivotal initiating experiences that arouse the "crisis of feeling" in us and invest vitality and conviction to our directed values, provide the basis for undertaking a study of politics — in the first place. The novel we are about to examine allows us to recapture the political initiating experience par excellence, i.e., the unwarranted arrest and execution of an innocent. It allows us to view the outrage from the standpoint of the victim.

Franz Kafka's *The Trial* is an extraordinary example of a novel that allows us to view the political scene from the standpoint of an individual undergoing a critical political experience. Kafka does not derive his politics from a doctrinaire party program, institutional investment, or from systematic theory. He takes his politics from the reverse side, i.e., from the standpoint of the innocent and uninitiated. He has the uncanny sense to look through the eyes of a victim who is caught unprepared and speechless. Kafka thus views the political institution from the obstructed perspective of those, who under the pressure of emergency, are most unable to cope with it. Kafka speaks through a man who knows practically nothing about politics; a man who therefore could not speak on his own problem. He evokes in continuous narrative the uncertain feelings and unsound ideation of an individual incapable of articulating his besetting political predicament. Kafka traces through his intimate medium the psychological duration of the political man in abstract who is suddenly and forcibly made aware of "his" concrete political condition. We obtain an evolving and elaborate picture of the man on the street who otherwise we see only in fragments and hear only in the isolated response of an interrupted interview.[18] Kafka thus places us at the receiving end of the political process and begins to unfold the tale from the position of the uninvolved and uninformed citizen.

When we turn to the opening page of a novel we are set to ask the author a number of preparatory questions: Where does this fictitious history occur? What is the time? Who are the critical characters?

This background information is perfunctorily submitted by the author because he is aware of the reader's need to establish a position and direction in the unfolding literary event. In thus specifying the spatial- temporal theater of action the novelist is providing the reader with a minimal orientation which will allow the latter to continue the journey through the body of the novel. But in so specifying the author is also drawing borders around the experience he is depicting and thus putting the reader at a certain distance. To be sure, it is the artist's task to transcend this specified boundary, already established, between his fictional world and the reader's personality. He thus constantly creates an obstacle he is trying to overcome. But this is a formidable task. Only the artist can put you outside his work and then seduce you back into it.

Kafka, by a bizarre and perhaps an unintended turn circumvents this fence between his characterization in *The Trial* and the reader. He leaves the historic context unspecified and does not recapitulate the past of his central character, Joseph K. He does not even permit us the modest certainty of his creature's family name! The three principles of orientation are thus conspicuously absent. The novel is in want of a time, a place, and an established character. Our initial inquiry is thus totally confounded. We have not been prepared by an introduction or a background. K. enters out of void, but notice the door has been left open. The actor's space has not been delimited so we may enter without trespassing. Before we are aware of our own self we are already in the shoes of the anonymous "K." We can immediately identify with him because he does not block us with an exclusive identity. We have at once become interchangeable with the character. We can endure his trial.

Politics as "If Not"

Joseph K. represents an innocent, unexamined existence. He has accepted his routine without struggle and has, indeed, escaped the problematic by an unwavering adherence to that routine. He is not in the least a riddle to himself and he does not seek out the riddle of the world. In fact, he rarely leaves his own neighborhood. The political authority at the fringe of his neighborhood is inaccessible and the nature of its operations has not been "brought home" to him. K. has accepted without provocative inquiry the publicly promulgated representation of the regime. Insofar as these images are commonly held and well known, no one is left uninformed by Kafka's refusal to recite them, but there is irony in this refusal. For in the stark obviousness and the patent acceptability of the common opinion the most critical deception is hidden. Kafka accentuates this irony by his unwillingness to express the collective cliches in recounting the life of his hero.[19]

Kafka has randomly selected K. from a vast citizenry of a nameless state. The selection is made at random because in Kafka's view any one individual in the "abstract mass" (Emil Lederer) exemplifies the orientation of all. The members are separate carriers partaking equally of the distributed abstractions current in their society. The members are as one in their minimal attention to the political environment, and this indifference facilitates the acceptance of unsupported assurances.

It is important at the outset to distinguish political apathy from political indifference. The latter characterizes Joseph K.'s position; the former does not. Apathy connotes the extinction or waning of a previous passion. Hence, the term indicates change or evolution of disposition, i.e., involvement to withdrawal. We speak of disillusioned radicals becoming apathetic. Indeed, apathy can even be understood in the heroic sense of overcoming or abandoning politics after profound and agonizing consideration. The apathetic man may know politics "all too well." Thus, apathy can conceivably specify both a low participation and a high awareness. Political indifference, on the other hand, is more of a static condition. It implies, as in the case of Joseph K., an absence of contact from the beginning. The uninitiated subject has never been responsive to the political institution and is, moreover, hardly aware of its presence.[20] Political indifference is thus characterized not only by a low participation, but also by low awareness. The citizen has never been in close quarters with the political institution and is thus innocent of it.

Joseph is one such "innocent" man. He lives in a country where the "rule of law" prevails, where constitutional protections are "in force," and the rights of privacy held inviolate. Yet "one fine morning" he is arrested without warrant or explanation. This arrest explodes K.'s easily owned assurances and assaults the "assumed protection" of K.'s citizenship. K. has become over-secure and is arrested in his "bedroom"

— caught in his "sleep."[21] K.'s political consciousness is enclosed by the briefest possible representations and he has assimilated to these comprehensive, if vaguely divined, symbols of "his" political organization, a motley collection of sensory associations.[22] K. has not given exacting attention to his political beliefs and often confuses differing levels of political contact. Indeed, this lack of discrimination is a precondition for the maintenance of his belief. Accordingly, K. can make, without qualm, grotesquely rigid political comparisons and distinctions, just because he has so little contact with actual processes of government. At the periphery of political life, he can arbitrarily pass judgment because there are no empirical deterrents in sight to force him to reconsider his abstract formulations.

Kafka tells us that K. obscurely receives news of political import as "rumor" from far off.[23] Joseph K. submissively receives these vague yet short-hand "rumors" without a thorough-going examination, not only because he lacks the critical capacities to go beyond them, but also because he rarely encounters the agents and only occasionally is involved in the "functions" of acting government. It is not difficult for K. to hold to this distorted picture of political authority because he is only in incidental contact with the "real thing." The few associations the citizen makes with political authority are those cursory encounters with agents in formal dress. This formal aspect of authority in the street only removes the citizen farther from the less pretentious but more cogent facts of exercised authority.

By identifying with the formal appearance the citizen is insulated from the disillusioning machinations of the government behind the daily scenes.[24] But the analogy with the drama applies only with a certain awkwardness. K. does not accept the difference between the real and the apparent in the government in the same way which he acknowledges the differences between the actual identity of an actor and the role he "make-believes." The billboarding, the staging, the costuming of the political performance does not impress K. as merely theatrical display. He takes it at face-value. K. does not presuppose that his government assumes the masked appearance of an omnipresent immortal guardian because it needs to "capture" an audience, and can best do so by a clever theatrical deception. In K.'s thinking, the promulgated images of the political institution represent the expected activity of government. Thus, the man on the street ceaselessly inflates his political expectations on the pump of sloganized assurances made in the street. All this is not an unfortunate accident. K. is systematically exposed to a performed appearance of government. The revealed aspect is what the man of the street sees in the street and nothing more. These permitted street-displays function as a barrier between the citizenry and the institutional operation. Concerning government, Bacon observed: it is like that part of knowledge which is secret and retired. In both these respects, certain things are kept secret not only because they are deemed impudent in speech, but also because they are hard to know and sometimes because they are not fit to utter. Therefore, we see all governments as obscure and invisible.[25] The regime, so to speak, must conceal its identity. This deceptive show of government is successful to the degree it is not recognized as deception.[26] The pretense can survive only as long as it remains undiscovered. Lessing advised the tragedian to "avoid anything that can remind the audience of an illusion (for as soon as they are reminded of the illusion it is gone)."[27]

The failure to perceive the dramatic illusion propagated in the public presentation of the political allows the citizen to act as if his fanciful expectations are unquestionably given. K. has these entrenched stereotypes reinforced every morning in his brief brush with authority in the outfit of the postman and policeman.[28] The uniform signalizes for him the omnipresence of the government in society and the immutability of its operation. In the first instance, the government appears overtly reliable to the citizen when he views the particular officer as a manifestation of the collective presence of an agency that appears to be at work everywhere. In the second case, he accepts the government as immortal because he notices that the failure or death of any single agent does not break the continuum. The legion automatically adjusts to the individual lapse and from the vantage of K. keeps on going — "forever."

K. places his trust with these costumed custodians of the political organization. Through K.'s adhesive reliance on this trust, he establishes not only his affected status of "belonging," but also partakes of the appealing dramatic illusion that can render that "belonging" choice-worthy. As long as K. is unaware of his presence in the political "theater" — as long as he cannot grasp the distinction between appearance and reality in the political — he can assume a guaranteed protection from the "omnipresent" and "immortal guardians." His position, by attachment to these non-existent attributes, thus becomes as unauthentic as the costumed performance generating these illusions. His assumed invulnerability is the correlative to K.'s belief in the regime's immortality. The poet advises, "Ruminate upon the belief and you shall fall into sleep."

K. places an exaggerated trust in the solidity of the political street-images and accordingly does not worry about them; reassured, he falls asleep, so to speak, in the comforting lap of the political authority. His unswerving faith in the protecting agents allows him to take his eyes off the institution. Thus, K. can put the government out of his mind insofar as he accepts its appearance without further thought. It thus assumes the status of an unexamined given, a matter of routine exclusion.[29] K. acts as if the government were not present in his neighborhood. Indeed, for K., the state has disappeared. But Kafka is not serving us a moral condemnation of K. Kafka does not expect his hero to possess in the first instance the insight, or the resilience, to face up to political facts of life. Kafka realized that an aroused awareness of the condition of government is intellectually exhausting and emotionally unbearable.[30] It is nothing less than painful for K. to examine his unyielding faith in this system of political appearance. K.'s political beliefs thus represent a systematic unconcern for "what is really happening." He can override contradictory perceptions by a tenacious routinization of his beliefs and, on the other hand, can routinize them just because he has no difficulty or stress in harboring them. "Of course, the deeper one digs one's pit the quieter it becomes; the less fearful one becomes, the quieter it becomes." Thus, K. has descended into his rut. He has excluded the novel events inherent in temporal change through a stultifying "habit of mind." "Habit," according to John Dewey, "enacts or overrides objects but it doesn't know them. Habits are too organized, too insistent and determinate to need to indulge into inquiry."[31]

Joseph K.'s attitudes toward the political institution has never seriously changed because they have never been subject to intense examination. The differential between his protected vision and the government's actual development only increases during his prolonged lethargy. But K. has slept too long, he has slept through critical changes which do not advantage his position. The appearances in this sleep have taken a sure hold on him. He is as certain of his safety in the political community as he is certain of the continuity of the processes of nature. He no more expects to be arbitrarily arrested than he expects it to snow in July. K. has become so completely habituated in the representation conveyed by political authority that these images circumscribe the limits of the natural in political life. The arbitrary violation of these limits is tantamount to an extraordinary interruption in the regularity of the processes of the physical world. K. has so zealously delimited and protected the politically "possible" by habitual adherence to the "forms" that any unexplained development is declared to be "unbelievable."[32]

The opening sentences of *The Trial* reveal at once the oncoming collapse of K.'s "possible" world and his single-minded refusal to give up the illusion on which it is based. "Someone must have been telling lies about Joseph K. for without having done anything wrong he was arrested one fine morning. His landlady's cook who always brought him his breakfast at eight o'clock failed to appear on this occasion. That had never happened before."[33]

K. will not admit the possibility of an unwarranted invasion by the authorities in the privacy of his daily doings. Such an admission presupposes the groundlessness of the arrest and the irrationality of the act committed by the representative of the government. This alternative, so alien to K.'s comfortable expectations, is "inconceivable." He immediately jumps to the conclusion that his warders have been deceived by "someone telling lies."

The government is not responsible for the unwarranted arrest; a malicious "someone" has falsely accused him and misguided the otherwise impeccable authorities. K. remains consistent to his expectations and in a studied calm requests a formal statement of the specific changes offered against him. The warder's response is shocking. "We are not authorized to tell you that." This flagrant violation of K. rights disposes K. to shift his suspicion from the "someone who tells lies" to the arresting warders. He is credulous of their representation. Only fakers would refuse to provide an explanation for such an extraordinary arrest. These men could only be frail impersonators for their pretense fails in one obvious respect — its legitimacy.

Who could these men be? What were they talking about? What authority could they represent? K. lived in a country with a legal constitution; there was universal peace; all the laws were in force; who dared seize him in his own dwelling?[34]

This action, falling outside the pre-established fence of the "believable," is assumed to be "make-believe." Thus, in a remarkable transvaluation the disillusioning is pictured as "make-believe." But it is necessary for K. to resort to this inversion because otherwise the "misrepresentation" becomes a massive and undeniable threat to K.'s very survival. It is needful, therefore, to interpret it as more than innocuous play at "make-believe." It is rather, in K.'s logic, merely another step to perceive his preposterous arrest as a grotesque practical joke. One could certainly regard the whole thing a joke, a rude joke which his colleagues in the bank had concocted for some unknown reason, perhaps because this was his thirtieth birthday. That was of course possible, perhaps he had only to laugh knowingly in these men's faces and they would laugh with him, perhaps they were merely porters from the street corner — they looked very like it.[35]

Thus, K. is readily prepared to be the butt of this "practical joke" as an alternative to accepting his arrest as a serious fait accompli.[36] K. will play the innocent victim and with secret irony he will turn the table on these jesters by countering their comic pretense with a counter-pretense of his own. None of his friends could then claim that "he could not take a joke"; he would have the last laugh. If this was a comedy, he would insist on playing it to the end. But K.'s elaborate self-deception is a pathetic groping for a facile and pacifying resolution that issues in a series of wild conjectures stretching the breaking point of his possible world. He allows his imagination unrestricted license in an attempt to exhaust all favorable alternatives and is carried to the bizarre extreme of constructing a make-believe world in which threats are taken as "practical jokes." He cannot drop his pretense, his part in the make-believe, but enters into it with the enthusiasm of a debutante.

K. "performs" in order to preserve the dramatic "illusion that "he was still free." At this point in the novel K. has been transformed into a "political actor" inasmuch as he now self-consciously represents the ideology of his paper constitution. K. refuses to accept the unequivocal challenge delivered by his warders, but flees to the fiction of "guaranteed" protection.[37] It is clear that K. has confused the meaning of "safeguard" and "guarantee." He does not conceive of his constitutional protection as a man-made fence subject to the inherent frailties of all human constructs, but imagines his rights "guaranteed" by the inalienable and insulated status he has won as a citizen. He has secured his civil rights by birth; hence his existence presupposes the impenetrability of his position. He takes his political rights for granted because he has been induced to believe that they are inextricably connected to the one fact he must take for granted: his existence. He takes his rights for granted in the same moment he takes himself for granted. Thus, K. hopes for a happy resolution of his present complication seem to be well-grounded. His expectations of a sanguine outcome in the future are irrevocably vouchsafed by the unqualified condition of his past, i.e., his birth. He may look forward without fear, because he may look backward for reassurance. The absoluteness of K.'s birth as an undergird for the inalienability of his rights appears to our hero as more than a tenuous, potentially collapsible safeguard; for him it assumes the enduring dignity of a "guarantee."[38]

Posturing with an assertive self-confidence, K. goes in search for "proof" of his identity. He could not find at first the identification papers for which he was looking. At last, he found his bicycle license and was about to start off with it to the warders, but then it seemed too trivial a thing and he searched again until he found his birth certificate.[39] His exaggerated faith in the forms is characterized by his reliance on "paper." He stakes his life on his bicycle license or his birth certificate! Kafka is caricaturing this confusion of credentials because he believes that neither one or the other can alter K.'s position. They are only "paper" guarantees and are only tokens of K.'s unsubstantial ground. But K. clutches his papers with conviction. He has proof that he exists!

K. believes that the status of his warders depends upon the authenticity of his papers, and that the official writ confirming his identity possesses the efficiency of a sacred talisman; to effect the withdrawal of the strange agents he has but to brandish his certificate. He boldly challenges: "Here are my papers, now show me yours, and first of all your warrant for arresting me." With the mock solicitousness of parading conquerors, the warders attempt to remind their reluctant victim of his grave predicament. "Oh, good Lord, if you would only realize your position and stop annoying us two, who probably mean better by you than any other people in the world."[40] But Joseph K. ignores their taunting admonitions and continues tapping his papers, repeating his incantation: "Here are my identification papers." But this prefabricated house of paper-safety receives a sudden blow in the tall warder's rage: What are your papers to us? You're behaving worse than a child. What are you after? Do you think you'll bring this fine case of yours to a speedier end by wrangling over papers and warrants? We are humble subordinates who can scarcely find our way through a legal document and have nothing to do with your case except to stand guard over you for ten hours a day and draw our pay from it. That's all we are, but we are quite capable of grasping the fact that the highest authorities we serve before they would order such an arrest as this, must be quite well informed about the reasons and the person of the prisoner. There can be no mistake about that. Our officials, so far as I know them and I only know the lowest grades among them are drawn toward the guilty and then must send out warders. That is the law.⁴¹

This frank admission of indifference and incompetence in the execution of the law — after the fact — from the lips of an agent of the law appears for K. as preposterous. What he had faithfully perceived to be the omnicompetent guardian of his rights is now glaringly represented as the authoritative enforcement of incompetence. For K. such a representation can only be received as an amateurish prank. Not only do these men act in arbitrary contravention of his legal position but they overtly deny and subvert the image of authority underlying that legal status by shameful admission. The whole scene in K.'s eyes is too "unbelievable" to be persuasive. Then in a presumptuous voice, he reveals his blissful remoteness from political reality! "I do not know this law,"⁴² declared K. in persistent defense of his ignorance, "and it probably exists nowhere but in your head." The warder replies: "See Willem, he admits that he doesn't know the law and yet he claims he's innocent."⁴³ This statement marks the watershed in K.'s development, for it carries an insight too telling to be refused. K. recognizes a weakness in his defense for the first time. His habituated image of the political structure is now presented to him as a creature of his ignorance and not on his presumptive opinion. The shock of recognition produced by this revelation of his naiveté revises the view K. holds of his position vis-à-vis the government.

Implicit in K.'s behavior, subsequent to this newly won, albeit dim, enlightenment, is the assumption that an individual's belief in his own innocence in no way compels the government's course of action. His trust in the fiction of his "guarantee," which implies at once his remoteness from the actual machinations of the authorities, becomes the mechanism by which his civil status is revoked. Thus, in sarcastic turnabout, K.'s warders wake him from the slumber of his dream world.⁴⁴ K.'s ignorance is declared to be the condition of his guilt.⁴⁵ He prepares his own arrest by excluding it, in the first instance, as a possibility. Thus, K. is the executive of the government's task inasmuch as he prefers to remain insulated and quiet.⁴⁶ Tyranny, in Kafka's thinking, is in no small measure, self-imposed. "The animal snatches the whip from its master so as to itself become master, and does not know that all this is only a fantasy caused by the new knot in the master's whiplash." The "myth" is mutually accepted by the control authorities and the mute citizenry. It is foisted from above; then it is admitted from below. Consequently, Kafka, in the strain of ironic neutrality that permeates the whole of the novel, suggests that the necessity to believe the "lie" is as great as the necessity to promulgate it.

K. recognizes his warders on their terms, but only after they have reminded him, in a toying paradox, that he cannot, without appearing absurd, remain ignorant of the law and in the same moment claim he is innocent. K. now realizes that he has been duped by his innocence, that his innocence is a naiveté. If the law is admittedly unknown to him, then perhaps these men represent what he does not know, that is, what goes on behind the appearances, the paper guarantees that he has uncritically taken for granted. If such is the case, then perhaps no one has lied or played a practical joke. Perhaps his arrestors are not frauds or impersonators. Perhaps they authentically represent the constituted authority. What he formerly dismissed as "impossible," he now discovers is actually close to the possible. He allows that his government can sanction illegal entry and can without warrant seize him in the sanctuary of his bedroom. Indeed, his government can erase, at will, the most critical distinction imprinted on his mind as a citizen — the distinction between guilt and innocence. The strict line between the two has now been confused.

K. has approached the insight that he has been deceived, caught in the scissors of self-deception and promulgated myth. The very admission of these possibilities already indicates that K. no longer excludes a priori the distressing alternatives posed by them. Preceding his arrest, K. was inclined to take things easily, to believe the worst only when the worst happened, to take no care for the morrow even when the outlook was threatening. Now that the "worst" has happened —K.'s arrest — he cannot move. His understanding of the situation cannot be of any service. It was too disturbing for K. to recognize the possibility of arrest prior to its arrival and then it is too late for effective action after it has become an irreversible condition. K. assumes the *bios politikos* only after he is victimized. He is aroused to the presence of the government when its manifestations appear disastrously obvious; but not before. The disconsolate irony is that Joseph K., the private citizen, becomes politically conscious only after he undergoes a trial. K. could know what he needed to protect only by suffering the loss of what he had taken for granted; but then it is too late. "The doorkeeper gave the message of salvation to the man only when it could no longer help him."[47]

The Breakdown of Political Identity

K.'s fictitious political world has gone to pieces and he acknowledges that he cannot expect justice form those who propagate the fiction. Indeed, he admits that "there can be no doubt that behind all the actions of this court of justice behind my arrest there is a great organization which not only enjoys corrupt warders, stupid inspectors and examining magistrates, but of whom the best that can be said is that they recognize their own limitations."[48] This disillusioning admission defines K.'s crisis. For if K.

allows for corruption, false influence, and stupidity in the political sphere, then he cannot save himself "merely" by invoking his constitutional rights. His arrest, he realizes, supervenes the question of his legal culpability.

Yet in his own defense, K. must continue to insist on his rights even if the effort is wasted: he has no alternative. But not only do the warders fail to provide cause for his arrest, but when he is admitted to interview with the more "sensible" inspector he is again refused an explanation. The recalcitrant inspector dismisses his request for a statement of charges: "I can't confirm that you are charged with an offense or rather I don't know whether you are. You are under arrest, certainly more than that I do not know."[49] K. importunes his arrestors to release him from the shadow of unspecified guilt, but the officers remain tight-lipped. K. cannot get beyond the brute fact of his arrest. His life is radically altered without explanation. The truncated dialogue and breakdown of the communicative link between K. and his wardens is a symptom of the general disintegration of K.'s civil status. K. does not receive even a cursory recognition of his expected rights against his extraordinary arrest.

K. is not accused of a specified crime and is consequently disallowed the protection of due process. He is suspended in a vacuum between categorical "guilt" and presumed "innocence." He is, thus, without recourse because he does not own a legal identity. Hannah Arendt has observed that it is paradoxically harder to kill the judicial person in a man who is guilty of some crime than in a totally innocent man. The stateless persons who in all European countries have lost their civil rights along with their nationality have learned this only too well; their legal position improved automatically as soon as they committed a theft: then they were no longer without rights but had the same rights as all other thieves. In order to kill the judicial person in man the concentration camp must under no circumstances become a calculable punishment for definite offenses.[50] Indeed, there is a tragic insight in Anatole France's famous quip, "If I am accused of stealing the towers of Notre Dame, I can only flee the country."

K. is disarmed of his self-defensive rights not because he has broken the law; for even in violation of the legal norm the criminal has resort to the minimal juridical defense and has the chance to resume his maximal status in society, i.e., the reestablishment of his civil rights. Even while being prosecuted to the full extent of the law he yet has access to the saving processes of the judicial network. But K. is set manifestly outside this supportive structure because his arrest is not based on a wrong legally defined. The calamity of the rightless is not that they are deprived of life, liberty and the pursuit of happiness or of equality before the law and freedom of opinion — formulas which were designed to solve problems within given communities — but that they no longer belong to any community whatsoever. Their plight is not that they are not equal before the law, but that no law exists for them — they remain perfectly "superfluous."[51]

K.'s predicament corresponds to the condition of "perfect superfluousness," a condition which leaves him completely helpless. Without refuge, K. is exposed to the unchecked invasion of the authorities. He, thus, begins a desperate quest for his legal identity in order to re-enter the sector of protection. This search takes him through the strange, unexplored terra incognita of the awesome judiciary "factory" and its accompanying bureaucracy. But it is only in examination of the "mysterious judicature" that he can discover the means to defend himself against it. K. assumes that his problem with the authorities, although more serious and unexpected in its impact and consequences, is akin to the routine difficulties he is called on to solve during the working hours at his bank. Certainly this is not an unreasonable assumption since it is based on the techniques employed in overcoming obstacles that impede the normal cycle of his day-to-day activities. If an individual is deprived of the means of existence to buy groceries it cannot harm him to inquire for a job to eliminate the problem presented by the gnawing in his stomach. If a painter is prevented from completing his composition by what he perceives to be a clash in color placement, he does not fear to improve on this harsh effect by turning to his palette to experiment with the available oils to produce a more satisfactory balance.

The attempt to solve these daily problems presupposes that inquiry, if not completely removing the disturbance, will at least not issue in compounded or insoluble difficulty. In common exchange one often hears this stated as, "you have nothing to lose by trying." Yet when K. makes his first overture to accept his problem as undeniably political in content and thus deserving of single-minded attention, he is "thrown into a certain agitation," and is threatened by his own questions: "Who accuses me?[52] What authority is conducting these proceedings?" He covers his fear with mock presumption: "I feel sure that after an explanation we shall be able to part from each other on the best of terms." The inspector responds in disgust, "You are laboring under a great delusion; these gentlemen here and myself have no standing in this affair of yours, indeed we hardly know anything about it."[53] The inspector blocks K.'s initial attempt to penetrate the represented authority by the subtle maneuver of turning the question back to its source, so as to undermine the responsibility of the questioner. If K. is thrown back on the rationale of his own questions he cannot begin to examine his arrestors; he can never go beyond the circular self-analysis of his own suspect motives. K. is vulnerable to this counter-questioning procedure because he has become pretentious under the pressure applied by his warders and is thus dubious of his own sincerity. He inflates his language to speak on their level, but he cannot take his performance seriously. Intimidated by the inspector's insidious advice, K. resumes his interior monologue: "Am I to be punished for my frankness by a rebuke? And about the cause of his arrest and about its instigator, am I to learn nothing?"[54]

K. continues to test the ground of his new experience and recognizes his own failure to control its development. He cannot keep the situation in hand because he lacks the authority to restore by his own works and influence the equilibrium of his "old course." The connection has been broken. He cannot make his inquiries effective because the object of inquiry will not submit to examination. The reluctance of the political representatives to give way to scrutiny is demonstrated by the systematic discourtesy of the inspector, who at once disavows any equality of status by refusing to shake K.'s hand.

K.'s attempt at interrogation is instantly stymied because he does not hold a position of equality vis-à-vis the authorities. He cannot wrest information from the inspector because he is the creature, he is the arrested — arrested in the literal sense; his motion is halted. Inquiry as an assertion of continued development and possible liberation is suspended by higher authority. The inability to cope with, let alone control, the consequences of his novel predicament is profoundly consternating for him. The failure of his questions to penetrate his arrestors leads him to the unwanted conclusion that the problem with the political is radically incommensurable with the problems he confronts and resolves in his daily regime.

K. has on his job and in the general run of domestic affairs sufficient resources at his command to overcome any obstacles that threaten to paralyze his schedules. He can in no way manipulate the components of the situation or reduce them to insignificance. He has lost control. He is "unprepared" to deal with the warders. Political questions confuse him and were more deeply embarrassing as he was obviously a man of the world who would have known how to comport himself anywhere else and would not have lightly renounced his natural superiority. Yet in this place he did not know even how to reply to a simple question.[55] He longs to return to the domain where his authority is unquestioned. "In the bank, for instance, I am always prepared, nothing of that kind could possibly happen to me there, I have my own attendant, the general telephone and the office telephone stand before me on my desk, people keep coming in to see me, clients and clerks, and above all my mind is always on my work and so kept on the alert, it would be an actual pleasure for me if a situation like that cropped up in the bank." Then with a sense for this bygone position of authority he resigns himself to his present predicament by saying: "Well, it is all past history now."[56] His business ingenuity is of no avail now because it is not allowed access, so to say, to the political market. This contrast of the plasticity and manageability of K.'s domestic affairs with the impenetrable and inscrutable aspects of the political sector reveals the exclusiveness of K.'s non-political life prior to his arrest. He is now bewildered before political authority because in the past he had discounted it, forgotten it was imminent in his environment.

K. cannot manage the course let alone work out the details of his political affairs. In default he is left with only a residual hope for a favorable resolution and this hope is undermined as the novel proceeds. He vainly seeks out the "high judge" to determine his status and resolve his case, but he is continually frustrated in this purpose and halted at the lower grade of the organization. His quest for the final authority to invest meaning in the whole "wild" affair is stymied. He is suspended, for all practical purposes, in the judicial bureaucracy. The political process leads into a blind alley.[57] The loss of the fictional picture of political authority, guarding him from birth, has not been replaced by a meaningful alternative structure. He has only a fragmented and isolated experience with ineffectual magistrates who can in no way determine his ultimate destiny. He is advised that the "judges of the lowest grade haven't the power to grant a final acquittal, that power is reserved for the highest court of all, which is quite inaccessible to you, to me and to all of us."[58]

Thus K.'s appointment with the determining authority is continually broken. He never obtains to the level of the high judge. If he makes a first step toward his advantage his progress is undone on the second step. "The whole dossier continues to circulate as the regular official routine demands passing on to the higher courts; being referred to the lower ones again — and thus swing backwards and forwards with greater or smaller oscillations, longer or shorter delays; these peregrinations are incalculable."[59] In spite of his determined effort K. has not advanced: the hierarchy breaks down as he tries to move up it. The ladder always collapses at the key rungs. K. tries to leap but consistently falls back cursing the concealed institution.

The commercial traveler who has suffered a parallel frustration advises: "It's very rarely that progress in these cases is visible at all. But I didn't know this. I was much more of a businessman than now, I wanted to see palpable results, the whole negotiation should be either on the upgrade, I thought, or on the downgrade and coming to a finish. Instead of that there were only ceremonial interviews, one after another, mostly of the same tenor where I could reel off the responses like a litany."[60] Nor was K.'s so-called advocate of any avail, for "strictly speaking, none of the advocates were recognized by the Court, all who appeared before the court as advocates being in reality merely in the position of hole-and-corner advocates."[61] They had become captive creatures of the administrative courts. "After acquiring an advocate I felt the stage was set for something to happen, and you did nothing whatever." The advocate replies, "after a certain stage in one's practice nothing new ever happens."[62] K. believes he is entering a "no-man's land" where nothing really happens. Thus when he is ushered into the political realm he believes he is caught up in a seemingly aimless institution.[63]

The organization appears "aimless" to K. because he is in no position to view it as a whole but only in inconclusive fragments. Suspended at the lower echelons he cannot obtain to the elevated, strategic standpoint of authority where these disconnected bureaucratic units can be seen as interdependent parts of an elaborate and well-concealed chain of command. In his blocked and isolated perspective, knowledge was only to be derived from a study of the various single stages of the case, but the single stages are not bridged and do not follow on each other in expected sequence. The trial does not develop in an orderly or cumulative fashion, and K. cannot therefore discover what is characteristically political. The organization lacks visible purpose, and uniform movement. K. sees it as an enormously complicated machine that does "nothing." The process appears in a continuing state of disintegration and in a manifest lack of function. K. cannot order his perceptions in this chaotic environment or make sense of the political experience. "Considering the senselessness of the whole, how is it possible for the higher ranks to prevent gross corruption in their agents."[64]

We now notice a remarkable transition in K.'s picture of the political. He is disabused as a result of his unwarranted arrest, of the fictitious presentation of authority. Nor can he rely on constitutional "guarantees" or the mechanism of juridical defense. The stereotyped guides that organized and directed his perceptions have been removed. Deprived of this perceptual support, K. is forced to pioneer through new ground with inexperienced eyes. The political activity is no longer represented to him in a coherent pattern.[65] It does not "give" to his unaided senses. K. has nothing but a series of separate interviews with innocuous bureaucrats which amount to an "exchange of useless admonitions." These fragmentary encounters are "not worth a penny at the final reckoning."[66] These bits of an incomplete puzzle are all he has to go on. He is no longer fed the political solutions, but must gather the facts by himself; but the data does not fall into a pattern and disallows legitimate inference. The political organization is inconceivably "mysterious" to him because he is a victim of unsupported, and dislocated vision. Thus he is disabused of his political presentiments only to fall victim to a peculiar political blindness. He exchanges one darkness for another. He is removed from the politics of deception only to fall into the politics of despair. When shocked into recognizing his disaster, he cannot substitute the awkward "facts" for the political fiction because he does not have recourse to an alternative standard of truth. He cannot gain political knowledge because he depended exclusively on false opinion for thirty years. Thus, when he finally wakes up in his moment of disillusion, he finds himself totally uninitiated in a wilderness of ungovernable perceptions. The loss of his fiction now forces him to depend on his own, naked and uninformed experience which he can acquire only piecemeal. Deprived of his pre-formulated picture, excluded from the common theater and denied legal status by his groundless arrest, he is at a complete loss.

Kafka describes the predicament of K. in another context. K. was once a part of the monumental group around some elevated middle part in which were ranged in carefully thought-out symbolic images — the military class, the arts, the sciences, the handicrafts. He was once one of the many. Now the group has long dispersed or at least he has left it and makes his way through life alone. He no longer has his old vocation indeed he has quite forgotten what he represented.[67] K.'s impotence in the political realm torments him. Thus, every hour that he spent away from the bank was a "trial to him."[68] "He shrank from being exiled from his work even for a single day."[69] His pre-eminent hope is to be able to circumvent his case, "a getting rid of it altogether," a mode of living completely outside the jurisdiction of the court. He longs to return to the comfort of a managed, secure home, to escape the enigmatic process going on in the political world. Politics makes him dizzy. He cannot stand the "air." The "fuggy atmosphere was unbearable" and later feels "as if he were seasick."[70] When he is allowed temporary leave from the administrative court, he leaps down the stairs, "so buoyantly and with such long strides he became almost afraid of his own reaction."[71] His striking "reaction" reveals his displacement in the unfamiliar institution. Politics is carried on at the periphery of his familiar world and it cannot but appear as unreal to him. He had never known it before. Now on contact he gets "dizzy" from the strange unmanageable pressures that impinge on him. he has never brought a sustained concern away from his private life to political affairs, and when he is finally forced into it, the ground is uncertain and unfamiliar. The authorities can turn his insular privacy to their advantage because, in his closed world, he is always off guard, always vulnerable. His fence collapses easily when they decide to break it down. On Thursday he was a well-established citizen. Friday, he is a helpless victim. Paradoxically, when the citizen insulates himself from the political realm in devotion to his personal affairs, he endangers, above all, this realm of privacy. By "staying indoors," remaining in prolonged isolation form politics, he is unprepared for and thus vulnerable to invasion. This "indoor" citizen is the opposite of a "look-out man" which is the meaning the Greeks gave to the word citizen (*polities*). K. looks into the political only after he is forced to do so, after his vigilance is useless.

The forced transition from the familiar associations of K.'s daily round to the unfamiliar "mysterious" ground of the massive political establishment prompts a desperate need for the dependable. He longs to return to the reality which is his home, his job, his neighborhood. These realities he can see and touch, depend on and reasonably control; but he cannot see, control or depend on the discontinuous bureaucracy of postponed interviews and inaccessible authorities. Nothing can be confirmed or disconfirmed in this "no-man's land." Nothing can be believed or disbelieved in this process without end-point,[72] and yet the bureaucracy is no less terrifying or potent because it is indefinite and anonymous.[73] Joseph K. no longer has a standard by which to judge the truth or falsity of the political representation. He is hopelessly confused; appearances are not what they seem to be. Yet it is not within the power of his unaided senses to locate the actual political determinants in back of the appearances. He does not find the face behind the mask. The government has confounded K. with fake offices, collapsible hierarchies, and deceiving magistrates. He cannot discriminate the shadow authority from de facto power. "You haven't once up to now come into real contact with our authorities. All these contacts have been illusory, but because of your ignorance of circumstances you take them to be real."

Thus, the paradoxical position of Joseph K., the citizen, "condemned not only in innocence but in ignorance" is evident from the beginning. It is not by accident that K., in the opening scene, is arrested in his bedroom, the sector of ultimate privacy, the palace of dreams. It is clear in the unfolding of his predicament that the bedroom as the limited domestic vicinity is tragically appropriate because it marks the boundary of his world. He is arrested there because he has never moved beyond it; his privacy is illusory because he assumed it was total and inviolate. Privation, is indeed, derived from the nuclear term privacy. He has suffered a privation of objective relationships with the environing political institution. His identity in the private is thus an illusory, precarious identity because it is based on a misapprehension of his own position.

This deception of total privacy renders K. totally defenseless — unprepared, an "innocent" victim. The impact of politics is "inconceivable" to him and is initially received by him as "nonsense."[74] He had not seen the institution with his "own eyes" and he cannot now believe it. Politics has been undisclosed to his senses (he has only been anesthetized by stereotypes). On actual contact he cannot understand it: "All the contacts have been illusory, but because of your ignorance of circumstances you take them to be real." Only after he is a captive, isolated in a "senseless" political world, does he recognize that the regime has turned "lying" into a universal principle. He is forced to "accept it as necessary."[75]

He is off balance, unsure and cannot find position in the systematic deception of the political process. He cannot regain his "innocence." When his civil status is destroyed, he not only loses his more general political identity, and the rights attached to it, but at the same moment loses specific identity based on his location in the "private". He has been displaced from the positions he always assumed were most unalienable: his profession, his neighborhood, his residence — he has lost his birthright, his name. No one can help him because no one recognizes him. Hannah Arendt, the profound observer of this condition of political estrangement observed: "The paradox involved in the loss of human rights is that such loss coincides with the instant when a person becomes a human being in general — without a profession, without a citizenship, without an opinion, without a deed by which to identify and specify himself — and different in general, representing nothing but his own absolutely unique individuality which, deprived of expression within and action upon a common world, loses all significance."[76]

Tormented by his exclusion from the "common world," K. is overcome by the pathetic delusion that someone is about to acknowledge him. Who was it? A friend? A good man? Someone who sympathized? Someone who wanted to help? Was it one person only? Or were they all there? Was help at hand? Were there some arguments in his favor that had been overlooked? Where was the high judge whom he had never seen? Where was the high court to which he never penetrated? He raised his hands and spread out all his fingers.[77]

But no one answers. No one sees him.

The Discontinuity of Political Life

In our age it is misleading to begin with the assumption that the man in the street (*homo communis*) is at once the political man (*homo politicus*). We distort the content of the former's experience by attributing to him the more specialized characteristics of the latter. The characteristic performances of the *homo communis* are not political acts.

Joseph K. represents the *homo communis* who is thoroughly accepted in his neighborhood but not visible in the political space. He does not act outside the domestic vicinity, and only vaguely recognizes the larger political organization which encompasses it. The peripheral institution does not "enter his mind." The absence of political authority in his daily life allows him to discount politics altogether. Kafka notices this disassociation and remarks: "The people believe the agents of the government have disappeared when actually they have only withdrawn to the edge of the city." But nonetheless, the people do act as if the government has disappeared, and this illusion permits the governed to pre-occupy themselves in the private space. The state has provisionally "withered away" for Joseph K. Indeed, the utopian dissolution of politics is no where so effectively accomplished as in the minds of the removed citizen. The states does not disappear by way of a deliberate extirpation of attachments. On the contrary, the citizen is hardly aware of its presence, so it could hardly threaten him. In such a situation there is no desire to destroy the political machinery; nor is there a wish to escape from it (there is nothing to escape from!). The citizen has merely ignored the political authority. Thus, Kafka says: "The exhausted population lives without a government until they hear the marching band or the voice of the tax assessor approaching the door."[78] Aside from these intermittent breaks, politics "doesn't happen" to Joseph K.

Max Weber remarked in his famous essay, "Politics as a Vocation": "We are all 'occasional' politicians when we cast our ballot or consummate a similar expression of intention. The whole relation of many people to politics is restricted to this."[79] Indeed, the body of the population is only politically activated on special occasions and can be counted only as they are involved during these periods. The occasions, to be sure, "incite great transient exertions," but they do not require a "continuity of effort." These periodic fits "may save the state in time of crisis, but often allow it to decline in time of peace." From this standpoint, the political institution is only necessary in a state of emergency and is only recognized at these extraordinary moments. However, the emergencies emerge only briefly until the citizenry are secure enough to resume slumber once more. When the veteran returns home, he is quite fed up with the conflict left behind. He turns the light off again and sleeps in isolation for another twenty years. He is only awakened at the onset of a crisis, a crisis that may well have capitalized on his sleep. Even at the lower order of discomfort, the private citizen cannot pay sustained attention to the political scene. He is quick to return to the more familiar, the "closer" contacts of the home and the neighborhood.

The political occasion is viewed by Kafka as a special interruption in the ongoing duration of the domestic continuum. The political institution becomes part of this immediate "vital environment" only at the arrival of cyclical celebrations, periodic elections and unexpected disasters. It is on these occasions that the impact of politics is temporarily, so to speak, brought "home" to him. Thus the state is preeminently associated with holidays and emergencies.

Kurt Riezler has observed: "The abstract mass at the receiving end of what we call mass communication is apolitical."[80] It appears strange that this apolitical man should yet be called "citizen." This specification of his political status seems altogether inappropriate in our time. Employed in the context of mass society the term "citizen" loses its denotative meaning. Indeed, it functions as a rhetorical expression and is used to whip an already inactive electorate. The voters at large are admonished to assume the responsibilities of citizenship because the fear is that the responsibility is not felt in the first place. Perhaps this is why the term sounds extravagant when it becomes current immediately before elections. It is often invoked as a last minute spur to prod those people to the polls who are not expected to show up. Accordingly, the hope is to prevent absenteeism by inducing a vague guilt in the individual for not living up to inflated expectations which the state has set for him. The franchise viewed in this context of political "nagging" is an uncomfortable "exercise" that is ritualistically performed. The right is not employed for any perceived purpose but is liquidated as an unwanted chore. Merriam and Gosnell in their classic book on non-voting tell us: "Citizens who vote only when they perceive some special, direct benefit derived therefrom are not likely to vote when the vision of that benefit is lacking. The men and women whose business or work engrosses most of their time were quite frequently indifferent toward elections, especially when their business had no very direct connection with the government."[81]

If the citizen votes when the vision of personal benefit is lacking, he does so with reluctance. He can hardly wait to complete the "task of the ballot" and resume the ongoing lethargy that preceded it. He has effectively evacuated the political arena and has left "that business" in the hands of strangers. The passive spectator does not independently initiate the political act but waits for prompting.[82] The political environment is not his element and on K.'s example is unnatural and uncomfortable. He finds himself out of place, "in the wrong building." This estrangement caught the acute insight of Adam Ferguson: "In proportion as territory is extended its parts lose their relative importance to the whole. Its inhabitants cease to perceive their connection with the state. Distance from the seats of administration and indifference to the persons who contend for preferment teach the majority to consider themselves as the subjects of a sovereignty, not as members of a political body."[83]

This condition has become even more widespread in the age of the mass society, and represents a fundamental break with the original understanding of citizenship. As derived from the Greek meaning, citizenship presupposed the conscientious participation and direct involvement of the individual on the functions of the body politic. Indeed, Aristotle tells us that a man cannot be considered a citizen unless he partakes of the deliberative and judicial offices of the state. Each man volunteers himself to the political task; "each citizen in his own assembly man; there is no bureaucracy worth the name."[84] The citizen makes the *polis* a part of himself in the same way that the craftsman makes a tool for himself. They count their minds most "truly their own when employed in behalf of the *polis*." According to Werner Jaeger every Greek citizen "belongs to two orders of existence because the polis gives each individual besides his private life a sort of second life, his *bios politikos*."[85]

In terms of the *bios politikos* and its participant functions, the citizens of the mass society are no citizens at all. Their political life is supported, so to speak, by artificial respiration. He or she does not himself partake of deliberative or judicial office, but "acts" only through a substitute, i.e., his representative.[86] Modern citizens are thus estranged from their political life because they do not finish their "own" act. Moreover, their substitute takes on an awe-inspiring symbolic role and hence "unknown" aspect to him. This seems to put them at a further distance. The citizen is represented by a stranger, and not by a relative or neighbor. He or she cannot casually meet his representative on the street or exchange intimacies over the fence. Thus, the political agents are not only geographically distant but inaccessible as "persons." This impenetrable, transpersonal pretense of political authority is the theme of the parable that immediately precedes the end of *The Trial*: "Before the law stands a doorkeeper on guard. To this doorkeeper comes a man from the country. But the doorkeeper says that he cannot admit the man at the moment. These are difficulties which the man from the country has not expected to meet. The law, he thinks should be accessible to every man at all times."[87]

When the actor is elevated to an authoritative role and thus set above the ordinary round to fulfill the extraordinary goals of the whole community, he is placed beyond the reach of the "man from the country." Charles Cooley has noted: "Authority, especially if it covers intrinsic personal weakness, has always a tendency to surround itself with forms of artificial mystery whose object is to prevent familiar contact and so give the imagination a chance to idealize."[88] The citizens are maintained in a state of mystification and awe only by regulating their contact with authority. Erving Goffman has elaborated this point in his brilliant book, *The Presentation of the Self in Everyday Life*:

> If we see perception as a form of contact and communion, then control over what is perceived is control over contact that is made and the limitation and regulation of what is shown is a limitation of regulation of contact. There is a relation here between informational terms and ritual ones, failure to regulate the information acquired by the audience involves possible disruption of the projected definition of the situation; failure to regulate contact involves possible ritual contamination of the performer.[89]

The political actors preserve their totemic distance by "acting" only in public. Their abstracted representation of a whole community of individuals prevents the disclosure of the private, intimate life. The uninitiated citizen on the other side of this regulated pretense cannot take these political representations as compelling and immediate demands just because they are kept at a remote distance from his pre-eminently moving, and intensely intimate concerns. The citizen cannot make politics a part of himself, as he can embrace the members of his immediate, innermost world. He does not have proximate contact with the political realm, and thus cannot control the processes which culminate in authoritative decisions. While he does not commit the actual political "act," nonetheless he plays the illusory role of citizen. It is only in the home and in the neighborhood that the man on the street owns the authority of speech and action. Indeed, what the man in the street can discuss without resorting to the cliches of ideology and the stereotypes of the public are his immediate contacts in his personal life. He can provide a detailed account of his job and its peculiar demands. He can describe the movements of his children and can depict his wife's eccentric tastes. He can disclose a rich variety of experiences within the domestic walls. But he is hard put to describe the functions of the judicial process. On such matters he is dependent on the summary uses of the mass media. The political arena is outside the realm of his immediate experience, so he receives his impressions second hand. He does not undergo the experience himself and consequently can take his "mind off" the political situation without suffering the "anxiety of absence" or the pangs of irresponsibility.

In fact, Joseph K. deliberately avoids getting "mixed up" in politics. After his arrest, he admits to one of the shadowed individuals in the administrative court: "I should never have lost an hour's sleep over the need for reforming the machinery of justice."[90] K. viewed political engagements not as a responsibility but as a violation — "interference with the machinery." On the one hand, he does not trespass, does not interfere in the political sector and, on the other hand, he acts as if the political authorities are forever excluded from his private space. The two spheres he presumes are incommensurable and exclusive. Each family becomes an organization in its own right, with its own private space. But because this space is more limited it also became more exclusive both physically and emotionally.[91]

Kafka appears to agree with Michels that the voluntary association is more a precipitate to smaller and exclusive friendship ties than a cohesive membership mediating to larger political and social organizations. "The people, like tardy arrivals, like strangers in a city, stand at some densely thronged side street peacefully munching the food they have brought with them, while away in front, in the market square at the heart of the city the execution of their ruler is proceeding." Thus, the man on the street is not wont to postpone his face-to-face conversation with his comrade or the immediate gratification of "the munching of the food" for the sake of the distant projects of the political organization.[92]

This "distance" of political authority is actually a myopic misapprehension of its actual proximity. It is necessary for Joseph K. to retain the distortion because he cannot integrate the *bios politikos* into his day-to-day existence. It has no felt impact on him nor is it associated with his spontaneous gratifications. The actual impact of the political institution is only appreciated after it delivers an immediate and undeniable threat. Thus, he is initiated into politics by his arrest.

The government enters "like a cold knife." Political authority can no longer appear at a distance, nor can it be "heard" as a muffled "rumor." It now assumes the painfully palpable effect of an open wound. The political presentation has "usurped his attention," and becomes his most vivid sensation.[93] He can no longer take the government in abstract because it is now an immediate and concrete threat to his survival. All of his time now is occupied with his reflections on the political consequences of his most petty acts. He is haunted by a sense of false privacy and expects the authorities to enter just when he engages in his most personal affairs. He is attuned in extreme to the presence of the government. In fact, he thinks of nothing else.

Although K. is not taken into custody, or incarcerated, but is allowed to move freely within the boundary of his civil vicinity, he cannot take his mind off his political predicament. The inspector advises: "You are under arrest, certainly, but that need not hinder you from going about your business. You won't be hampered in carrying on in the ordinary course of your life."[94] But K. cannot "carry on" in the ordinary course of his first life, and it consequently wastes away from inattention.

K.'s arrest forces a total reverse of his old life, which was characterized by a singleminded preoccupation with private space and a complete lack of attention to the political environment. He now speaks in the rhetoric of his arrestors. Joseph K. is thus helplessly driven from one extreme to the other. He cannot negotiate between the political and non-political sectors because he cannot objectively evaluate their impinging pressures. In the end, he cannot overcome the fundamental dissociation of his history.

The *homo communis* and the *homo politicus* are divided against him. K. cannot compose the two orders of existence and thus loses both. His execution merely confirms the fatal division in himself.

Notes to A Political Interpretation of Franz Kafka's *The Trial*

1. It becomes clear in the review of Kafka criticism that it is just the provisional indeterminate status of Kafka's literature that inspires in his interpreters a compelling need for certainty. But according to Kafka, every thought dies when it is enclosed.

2. Walter Kaufman, *Existentialism from Dostoevsky to Sartre* (New York: Meridian Books, 1957), p. 122.

3. *Diaries* (New York: Schocken Books, 1948), p. 249.

4. Kaufman, op. cit., p. 122.

5. G. E. Moore, *Philosophical papers* (London: G. Allen & Unwin, 1959), p. 224.

6. J. A. Creighton, "Reason and Feeling," *Philosophical Review*, XXX, No. 5 (1921), 469.

7. Fritz Stern, ed., *The Varieties of History* (New York: Meridian Books, 1956), p. 142.

8. Hannah Arendt, "Understanding and Politics," *Partisan Review*, XX, No. 4 (1953), 378,

9. Bergson was singularly aware of the attenuation of "real duration" by the spatial dimension of history. "By the very fact of breaking up concrete time we set out its moments in homogeneous space. The only step then remaining will be to describe figures in space, to make them move according to mathematically formulated laws, and to explain the apparent qualities of matter by the shape, position and motion of these geometrical figures." *Time and Free Will*, trans. F. L. Pogson (London: Macmillan, 1910), p. 212.

10. F. H. Bradley, *Appearance and Reality* (Oxford: Clarendon, 1946), 10th impression.

11. Marcel Proust, *Remembrance of Things Past* (New York: Random House, 1927), II, 996.

12. Ortega y Gasset, "Notes on the Novel," in *The Dehumanization of Art and Other Writings* (New York: Doubleday Anchor Book, 1957), p. 84.

13. *Works*, ed. by William Archer (New York: Scribners, 1911), IV, 199.

14. *The Course in Poetics: First Lesson, tr. by Jackson Mathews, Southern Review*, Vol. VI, No. 3 (Winter, 1940).

15. *Principles of Psychology* (New York: Henry Holt & Co., 1899), I, 141.

16. We enter more readily into sentiments which resemble those we feel everyday; but no passion when well represented, can be entirely indifferent to us; because there is none, of which man has not, within him, at least the seeds and first principles." David Hume, *An Enquiry Concerning the Principles of Morals* (London: Open Court, 1913; reprinted from edition of 1777), p. 57.

17. *The Magic Mountain* (New York: Harcourt, Brace & Co., 1928), p. 66.

18. In taking the position of the uninitiated, Kafka speaks in the impeded tongue and is faithful to the unresponsive silence of his "unheroic" hero. He never avoids the description of Joseph K.'s struggle with petty problems because these struggles characterize his unabstracted movements in his own neighborhood.

19. The abbreviation K signifies both the barrenness of Kafka's character and Kafka's reluctance to go beyond the barest analysis of the self-evident life. Only when the extraordinary impact of the arrest overthrows the "appearance" of his life does K. take on psychological dimension. It is then that he is given life because only at that moment does he commence self-exploration. Indeed, *Der Prozess* connotes more than the controlled legal position. It also suggests the submission of self to examination. (I undergo the process. I put myself on trial). Kafka intersects the political meaning with a profoundly psychological one: As soon as one is forced into self-examination, there is no escape from self-accusation. K. cannot prove his innocence once he begins to question himself.

20. For an outstanding example of this confusion of apathy and indifference, see Morris Rosenberg, "Some Determinants of Political Apathy," *Public Opinion Quarterly*, XVIII (Winter, 1954), 349-66.

21. It is kind of terrifying irony that fifteen years after Kafka's novel was written Robert Ley could mock: "The only person who is still a private individual in Germany is somebody who is asleep." *Dictatorship and Political Police: The Technique of the Controlling Fear* (London: Secker Warburg, 1945), p. 178.

22. The symbol prevents the observational and intellectual process, the observer gets drawn into his objects. Fascinated and even awe-inspired by them, and they evoke in the end the whole conscious activity until he is eventually "thrown together" into a unity. Michael Fordham, *New Developments on Analytical Psychology* (London: Routledge and Kegan Paul, 1959), p. 61.

23. Allport and Postman have noticed that rumor circulates in proportion to the ambiguity of the subject matter and "as it travels, tends to grow shorter, more concise, more easily grasped and told." *Psychology of Rumor* (New York: Henry Holt, 1947), p. 15.

24. "The private citizen today has come to feel rather like a deaf spectator in the back row who ought to keep his mind on the affairs are in no way his affairs. They are for the most part invisible. They are managed, if they are managed at all, at distant centers from behind the scenes by unnamed powers. He lives in a world which he cannot see, does not understand and is unable to direct." Walter Lippman, *Phantom Public* (London: Macmillan, 1925), pp. 13-14.

25. Francis Bacon, *The Advancement of Learning* (London: J. M. Dent, 1934), p. 204.

26. Compare Alexander Koyre, "The Political Function of the Modern Lie," in *Contemporary Jewish Record*, June, 1945.

27. *Laocoon*, translated by E. Beasley and H. Zimmern (London: G. Bell and Sons, 1888), p. 87.

28. Isidor Ginsburg in his discussion of German national symbolism observes: "The governmental official wears a certain uniform; coins and postage stamps bear the state insignia; there are public buildings and monuments. More important by far is the fact that every time the individual comes into contact with government, it is through some visible, concrete person, institution or organization which symbolizes the invisible, intangible but very real and powerful institution, the state. *Modern Germany: A Study of Conflicting Loyalties* (Chicago: University of Chicago Press, 1933), p. 295.

29. William James tells us that, "habit depends on sensations not attended to." *Principles of Psychology* (New York: Henry Holt, 1915), p. 141.

30. "When the complexity becomes intolerable it (the imagination) retreats into symbolic images. We have an intense hatred of multi- dimensional value orderings." Kenneth Boulding, *The Image* (Ann Arbor: University of Michigan Press, 1956), p. 119. Jacques Hadamard has also observed: "The laws of tense thought (intellectual work) may be and seem to be very different from those of usual and common ideation, which is the only frequent one among ordinary people." *The Psychology of Invention in the Mathematical Field* (Princeton: Princeton University Press, 1945), p. 87.

31. *Human Nature and Conduct* (New York: Modern Library Edition, 1930), p. 117.

32. Czeslau Milosz reflects that "man tends to regard the order he lives in as natural. The house he passes on his way to work seems more like rocks rising out of the earth than like products of human hands. He considers the work he does in his office or factory as essential to the harmonious functioning of the world. The clothes he wears are exactly what they should be and he laughs at the idea that he might equally well be wearing a Roman toga or medieval armor. He cannot believe that one day a rider may appear on a street he knows well, where cats sleep and children play, and start catching passersby with his lasso." *The Captive Mind* (New York: Alfred A. Knopf, 1955), pp. 24-25.

33. *The Trial* (London: Secker and Wearburg, 1950), p. 10. Translated by Willa and Edwin Muir.

34. Ibid., p. 10.

35. Ibid., p. 11.

36. Erik Erikson has noticed: "When threatened with such anxiety, we either magnify a danger which we have no reason to fear excessively — or we ignore a danger which we have every reason to fear." *Childhood and Society* (New York: W.W. Norton, 1950), p. 363. K. denies the real threat for fear of the consequences of recognizing it.

37. "It is the immutability of a citizen's status that makes the person feel secure in the ideology, come what may, he belongs." Sebastian De Grazia, *The Political Community* (Chicago: University of Chicago Press, 1948), p. 89.

38. Roscoe Pound has recognized that "in the encroaching absolutism constitutional guarantees are guarantees of phantoms." *Social Control through Law* (New Haven: Yale University Press, 1942), p. 96.

39. Kafka, op. cit., p. 11.

40. Ibid p. 12.

41. Ibid., p. 12.

42. Ibid., p. 13.

43. Ibid., p. 13.

44. "The infantile state of the mass man is so unrealistic that he never thinks to ask who is paying the price for his paradise." C. G. Jung, *The Undiscovered Self* (New York: Mentor Books, 1957), p. 72.

45. K., to be sure, is not guilty on the regulatory postulate, *ignorantia legis neminem excusat*, because he is not ignorant of any established law that he has unwittingly broken. Indeed, his arrestors violate the juridical rule, no crime except by legal definition (*nullum crimen, nulla poena sine lege*). His ignorance is not

criminal in the specific legal context, but he is nonetheless "guilty" in the larger sense of remaining totally detached from his political situation.

46. "Democratic government rests as much on the silent approbation and tolerance of the indifferent and inarticulate sections of the people as on the articulate and visible institutions and organizations of the country." Hannah Arendt, *The Origins of Totalitarianism* (New York: Harcourt, Brace and Co., 1951), p. 306.

47. Kafka, op. cit., p. 236

48. Ibid., p. 54.

49. Ibid., p. 18. Alex Inkeles has remarked in this context: "The (totalitarian) regime seeks to create in every man the nagging feat that he may have done something wrong, that he may have left something undone — it is an important part of the pattern that he be unable to find out with certainty whether he actually did err or not." "The Totalitarian Mystique" in *Totalitarianism*, edited by Carl J. Friedrich (Cambridge: Harvard University Press, 1954), pp. 106-7.

50. Hannah Arendt, "On the Concentration Camp," *Partisan Review*, XV, No. 7 (1949), 752.

51. Hannah Arendt, *Origins of Totalitarianism*, p. 293.

52. Kafka, op. cit., p. 19.

53. Ibid., p. 18.

54. Ibid., p. 19.

55. Ibid., p. 74.

56. Ibid., p. 27.

57. This attempt to achieve ultimate solution or final determination in an indeterminate situation is viewed by Kafka, as the "most aggressive, if futile human aim." "No one can lead the way to India. Even in Alexander's time, the gates were beyond reach, but their direction was indicated by the King's sword. Today these gates have been moved somewhere else, farther away and higher up; no one indicates the direction." *The Kafka Problem*, ed. Angel Flores (New York: New Directors, 1946), p. 264.

58. Kafka, op. cit., p. 173.

59. Ibid., p. 174.

60. Ibid., p. 194.

61. Ibid., p. 128.

62. Ibid., p. 204.

63. Ibid., p. 169. This apparent "aimlessness" can also be seen as a calculated attempt to confuse the uninitiated and thereby keep the de facto organization secret. See also Max Weber, "The concept of the official secret is the specific invention of bureaucracy." H. H. Gerth and C. Wright Mills, "Bureaucracy," *Essays in Sociology* (Cambridge: Oxford University Press, 1946), p. 233.

64. Kafka, op. cit., p. 206.

65. Allen Wheelis, in describing this anxiety, states that the complex institutions "are not a trackless waste but the tracks are so numerous, so winding, so superimposed on one another, that no man can find his way with certainty." *The Quest for Identity* (New York: W. W. Norton, 1958), p. 187.

66. Kafka, op. cit., p. 116.

67. *The Great Wall of China* (New York: Schocken Books, 1956), p. 36.

68. Kafka, op. cit., p. 216.

69. Ibid., p. 217.

70. Ibid., p. 82.

71. Ibid., p. 84.

72. Bertram Wolfe remarks that the "hero of Orwell's Nineteen Eighty-Four feared that he was going mad when all the objective landmarks by which he might get his bearings began to shift and crack and change into independable and unrecognizable shapes." Quoted in "Totalitarianism and History," *Totalitarianism*, edited by C. J. Friedrich (Cambridge: Harvard University Press, 1954), p. 273.

73. Hannah Arendt observes: "As we know from the most social form of government, that is, from bureaucracy (the last stage of government in the nation-state just as one-man rule in benevolent despotism and absolutism was its first), the rule by nobody is not necessarily no-rule; it may indeed, under certain circumstances, even turn out to be one of its cruelest and most tyrannical versions." Quoted in *The Human Condition* (Chicago: The University of Chicago Press, 1958), p. 40.

74. The fracture of identity under radical stress in an extreme political situation was described by Bruno Bettelheim: "This cannot be true, such things just do not happen. . . . The prisoners had to convince themselves that this was real, was really happening and not just a nightmare. They were never wholly successful." "On Dachau and Buchenwald" in *Nazi Conspiracy* (Washington: U. S. Government Printing Office, 1947), VII, 824.

75. Kafka, op. cit., p. 243.

76. Hannah Arendt, *The Origins of Totalitarianism*, pp. 297-98.

77. Kafka, op. cit., p. 251.

78. *Diaries* (New York: Schocken Books, 1948), p. 249.

79. *Essays in Sociology*, tr. by. H. H. Gerth and C. Wright Mills (Cambridge: Oxford University Press, 1940), p. 83.

80. "Political Decisions in Modern Society," in *Ethics*, January, 1954 (Chicago: University of Chicago Press), p. 47.

81. Charles E. Merriam and Harold F. Gosnell, *Non-Voting* (Chicago: University of Chicago Press, 1924), p. 167.

82. Ritual participation which demands no more than reflexive consent degenerates into the "plebisciterian democracy." At this point participation has lost its deliberative function and is turned against itself. Morton Grodzins has rightly observed: "To whip up, certainly to enforce, participation is to endanger democracy. Those who enforce participation must in the end dictate to the participants." *The Loyal and the Disloyal* (Chicago: The University of Chicago Press, 1956), p. 249.

83. Adam Ferguson, *An Essay on the History of Civil Society* (Edinburgh, Scotland: Bell and Bradfute; William Creech; Manner and Miller, 1814), p. 454.

84. Riezler, op. cit., p. 11.

85. *Phaideia* (Oxford: B. Blackwell, 1939), I, 111.

86. The Greek verb "to act" (*prattein*) connotes "to pass through" or "to finish." In this sense, the modern citizen does not commit a political "act" because it is mediated and finished by someone else, i.e., the representative. (See Arendt, op. cit., p. 189).

87. Kafka, op. cit., p. 235.

88. Charles Cooley, *Human Nature and the Social Order* (New York: Scribners, 1922), p. 351.

89. *Presentation of the Self in Everyday Life* (New York: Doubleday: Anchor Books, 1959), p. 67.

90. Franz Kafka, *The Trial*, p. 60.

91. Compare with the remarks of Thorstein Veblen: "So far as concerns that portion of their consumption that may without blame be carried on in secret, they withdraw from all contact from their neighbors. Hence the exclusiveness of people, as regards their domestic life, in most industrially developed communities." *Theory of the Leisure Class* (London: Macmillan, 1924), p. 112.

92. Lasswell has observed in this context: "Stresses arising from everywhere in the personality systems can be disposed of by bodily movement, autistic fantasies, critical reflections any new expedient of tension removal can be stereotyped and repeated. Hence, the political symbols must compete with all the channels of autistic and somatic release for the control of personal energies." *World Politics and Personal Insecurity* (New York: McGraw Hill Book Co., 1935), p. 133.

93. Kafka, op. cit., p. 21.

94. Ibid., p. 21.

BIBLIOGRAPHY

Allport, Gordon W. *Basic Psychology of Rumor.* New York: Henry Holt and Company, 1947.
Arendt, Hannah. *The Origins of Totalitarianism.* New York: Harcourt, 1951.
The Human Condition. Chicago: The University of Chicago Press, 1958.
Bacon, Francis. *The Advancement of Learning.* London: J. M. Dent and Company, 1934.
Bradley, F. H. *Appearance and Reality.* Oxford: Clarendon Press, 1946.
Cooley, Charles. *Human Nature and the Social Order.* New York: Scribners and Company, 1922.
De Grazia, Alfred. *The Political Community.* Chicago: The University of Chicago Press, 1948.
Dewey, John. *Human Nature and Conduct.* New York: Modern Library, 1930.
Erikson, Erik H. *Childhood and Society.* New York: W. W. Norton and Company, 1950.
Ferguson, Adam. *An Essay on the History of Civil Society.* Edinburgh, Scotland: Bell, Bradfute, Creech, Manner and Miller and Company, 1814.
Fordham, Michael. *New Development in Analytical Psychology.* Routledge Kegan Paul, 1959.
Goffman, Erving. *The Presentation of the Self in Everyday Life.* New York: Doubleday Anchor Books, 1959.
Grodzins, Morton. *The Loyal and the Disloyal.* Chicago: The University of Chicago Press, 1956.
James, William. *The Principles of Psychology.* New York: Henry Holt and Company, 1913.
Kafka, Franz. *The Description of A Struggle.* New York: Schocken Books, 1948.
The Diaries. New York: Schocken Books, 1948.
The Great Wall of China. New York: Schocken Books, 1948.
The Trial. London: Secker and Warburg, 1950.
Lasswell, Harold. *World politics and Personal Insecurity.* New York: McGraw Hill , 1935.
Lessing, Gotthold. *Laokoon.* London: G. Bell and Sons, 1888.

Lippmann, Walter. *The Phantom Public*. New York: Macmillan and Company, 1925.
Mann, Thomas. *The Magic Mountain*. New York: Harcourt, Brace and Company, 1928.
Milosz, Czeslau. *The Captive Mind*. New York: Alfred Knopf, 1955.
Moore, George E. *Philosophical Papers*. London: G. Allen and Unwin, 1959.
Ortega y Gasset, Jose. *The Dehumanization of Art and Other Writings*. New York: Doubleday Anchor Books, 1954.
Pound, Roscoe. *Social Control Through Law*. New Haven: Yale University Press, 1942.
Rochefort, Robert. *Kafka, ou L'irreductible espoir*. Paris: Julliard, 1947.
Veblen, Thorstein. *The Theory of the Leisure Class*. London: Macmillan, 1924.
Wheelis, Allen. *The Quest for Identity*. New York: W. W. Norton, 1958.

The Theater

(1961)

(*Phoenix*, Fall 1961, pp. 13-14).

Members of the audience, my dear patrons: I have a regrettable announcement to make: due to circumstances beyond my control I will not be able to perform for you tonight. Yes, I am deeply sorry, I sympathize with your disappointment, but there is nothing to be done. We cannot go on. Yes, I know you've come a long way and I appreciate the sacrifices you have made to attend, but let this be a lesson to you: always prepare for an unexpected cancellation. No, my good woman, your ears are not failing; the program has been cancelled until further notice. I realize that you have been waiting patiently in the lobby for the aisle doors to open. Unfortunately none of you will gain entry. The doors, under strict orders, will remain closed. Now let us not create a disturbance, but in the spirit of polite theater-going turn about and leave the premises in good form; do not bother to look back as you make exit — keep moving out. No, I can't be bothered by tickets — out — get out.

Wait a minute! Heaven knows I would not choose to alienate your good will but would prefer to stay with you awhile to give you satisfaction for your tickets. But all ... everything is foreclosed. I am helplessly preoccupied with another audience. Indeed, they have appropriated your seats, the seats reserved for you.

It is the group within me, now being seated.

To be sure, these internal patrons were not escorted to their seats according to procedure but they trampled on the ushers, and are now on their way to get into the performance. They are taking over the show. Excuse me for shouting, but I can hardly hear myself speak for the din.

I should have known better: an audience always wishes to usurp the role of the performer: Bring down the actor! Steal his scene. Indeed, a player is never safe from the audience in the balcony of his mind. They have descended without warning, unleashing their hidden emotion and I must bow before them, pre-empted of any commitment to you. Oh the outrage, shameless reversal of the natural order: Your speaker, master of the art, becomes captive of his own audience.

I am in full retreat. They have blocked my saving exit — the stage door. Almost as if my back were at the wall, at complete disadvantage, I can do nothing but capitulate; nor will I save face in the surrender; for the terms are calculated to taunt me in defeat. The provisional committee demands that I now take orders from them, become their creature, or sever my relation with the theater altogether.

Surely the wretches know full well that the latter alternative is no alternative at all, that I cannot exist outside the theater. After all what am I but my matinee and evening performances?

It is obvious that they intend to split me from my role, to annihilate my history as an actor, cancel me out to a remainder. They have re-auditioned me for a role I had made famous. Moreover it is part of their diabolical game to invent faults in characterization heretofore hailed as flawless.

During any phase of my performance I can be arbitrarily interrupted by the provisional committee. Interrupted, chastised, humiliated, for overstepping the constricted boundary of my role. Extemporized! Deviated from the script! Modulated: a suspect inflection in the voice. I am guilty of subversive virtuosity and I recant — according to the dictates of the script.

Please forgive my cowardice in this affair, but you must remember that there is no appeal to an alternative audience. My histrionics can hardly be appreciated when no one is listening and if there is no response to my heroics, why should I suffer martyrdom? Tell me, what is more ludicrous than a wasted enthusiasm, a Hamlet in an empty house? But of course I do not mean to say that no one ever hears. "They" are always listening, taking notes and laughing.

Released to their own rhythm by the license of their new authority, my auditors have moved behind the scenes and now mock me from the wings. They are stationed on the wrong side of the footlights to gain the ironical advantage of viewing me from the rear. I am, thus, performing to an audience that is continually behind me.

Unfortunately, I cannot but appear ridiculous from backstage. The group can watch me unravel my most casual gestures by a deliberate counting, observe how I schedule my spontaneous outbursts, rehearse my enthusiasm. They are inconstant vicinity of my deception and relish pointing out my systematic insincerity. When I purpose to reach the high point of my soliloquy, they are prompted to the most derisive laughter. If I attempt to invest a tragic tone in my perfunctory recitation, they irreverently goad me with the strains of plastic violins. If I burst through my scripted mechanics with an authentic tear, they regurgitate hysterical giggles. Whenever I begin a mood, they crush it.

It all amounts to a spiteful refusal to take me at face-value; and I must bear this degradation in humiliated silence, a helpless bystander at the dispossession of my own estate.

But now hear: in spite of the dangerous proximity of the internal membership, I will open the small corner of my mouth for you, taking the risk, to reveal a secret in a whisper which is not, of course, for them. Can you hear me? Good. Now in my heart of hearts I am convinced that you my loyal friends of the lobby are a more sympathetic part of me than my own group. Indeed I have more in common with the audience on the out than the ensemble within. You, at least, take at face; and mutual face-acceptance is the tightest public bond.

That is the chain that links all our rouged cheeks and girdles us in cosmetic community. They have seen my make-up streak. The face drips off and is then replastered. There is not a part of me that cannot be removed nor a pretense that cannot be assumed. It all depends on the make-up.

"Take if off, take if off," shout the boys in the rear. Always one step ahead, always waiting for me when I return to my dressing room, with their hats held over malicious hearts: "We are here to celebrate your moving performance." And this sarcastic nicety is fused to an explosive, dissonant rant: "You are not a man but a series of layers, a sequence of costumes; you are not a face but an infinite regression of masks; and your words - a counterfeit currency issued on a market of negotiable lies."

Between this mockery and the lobby-doors, there is only an applauseless silence. And on the barren stage, a platformed island, I stand condemned for what I seem to be. And you, my devotees beyond the doors, cannot save me. You cannot come in and I cannot go out. We can no longer accommodate our faces nor play the flattering mirror to each other. I will never appear before you again except in your memories, and those revivals, I suspect, will become ever more infrequent. Your speaker, as of this moment, is a "has-been" - having been an actor and nothing more.

Even now I distrust my presence. Am I here? Do I speak? Have I performed my life away, forgotten it between bows, lost it somewhere on stage — but where? Where? I hear the group within me laughing.

It is too late to recover. The theater is closed and I with it.

Brotherly Interlude III

In one of his rare published gems, Jerry employed the term "discourse" in the sense that Foucault used it and long before the Foucauldians made it a key component of the fashionable vocabulary of postmodernism. Even more startling is his introduction of the idea of the "omniscient spectator" who fulfills the need for a transcendental signified to certify the shaky grounds upon which all intellectual enterprise rests. Postmodernists followed Jerry in going after the omniscient author-legislator who made universal truth-claims and prescriptive pronouncements. Jerry's study of Sorel's attack on the Enlightenment and bourgeois rationalism reinforced his own native tendency to challenge the epistemological assumptions and methodological conventions of academic disciplines. In the following paper, Jerry questions the unseen "authority" on which the social sciences depend and which encourages predetermined answers. His spirited inquiry is studded with those vivid similes and metaphors that made his everyday conversation so riveting.

DOES POLITICAL DISCOURSE HAVE A LIMIT?

(1964)

(*The Western Political Quarterly*, supplement, vol. 17, 1964, pp. 132-133)

That science would naturally seem to be the most sovereign of the sciences — the science which is most of a master-science. Now politics appears to be of this nature" (Aristotle's *Ethics*).

We have been trained to think of politics as the architectonic science, the associations, *the* map of maps. But think of Chinese boxes, a smaller one contained in a larger one and that one included in an even larger one *ad infinitum*. The claim of political science subjects it to a comparable regress. For an inquiry into the *sovereign* and *inclusive* association cannot be restricted. We can always ask again with significance: Who governs *the* sovereign? What authorizes the authorities? Kant perceived this logical difficulty in the study of human affairs but cast it in ethical terms: "The difficulty of which the mere thought of this problem puts before our eyes is this. Man is an animal which, if he lives among others of his kind, requires a master. But whence does he get his master? Only from the human race. But the master is himself an animal and needs a master."

Although Kant faces the dilemma of "mastery", he uses the term ambiguously. He confuses the two distinctive logical levels of this term. The primary statement of "mastery" refers to specific relations between individuals, e.g., "Eumaeus is the obedient swineherd of Ulysses." But mastery is also employed in statements of a second or higher logical range referring to relations of classes to subclasses of individuals — "The state governs the provinces." Louis the Fourteenth and the French Nation are not "master" of the same logical type, even though the deceptive plasticity of language confounds them.

Now the use of mastery in the second order, as a class concept, is characteristic of political thought. But one cannot claim the ultimate for a class of classes, for it again can be subsumed in a larger class. How, then, can we assert the limits of an ultimate association without speaking in paradoxes? We cannot master the meaning of "master." For how do we define rules for, and play a game upon, an unlimited field?

Political discourse attempts to surmount this difficulty by introducing what might be called the fiction of the *omniscient spectator*, for only omniscience can halt the infinite expansion and "mark" the boundaries. (This fiction represents the fusion of different logical types. Consider the classic example of the "general-will." An attribute of classes is illegitimately mixed with an attribute of individuals.)

The pronounced resemblance of political to theological discourse is instructive here. The language of politics is fashioned for a deity who "sees" through the infinite series, who comprehends and completes the affairs of men. Thus Bolingbroke could assert that the "pleasures of statescraft are like those attributed to a supreme being on a survey of his works." Sovereignty is predicated of Gods and divinity is attributed to sovereigns.

These mixed usages only disguise the problem of analysis. For society is inhabited by men and we do not share our responsibilities with an *omniscient spectator*. Wittgenstein notes "even for God the mere rule of expansion (for *pi*) cannot decide anything that it cannot decide for us." (*Remarks on the Foundations of Mathematics*.) Omniscience cannot overcome a logical impasse. Thus when we give an instruction to treat politics as architectonic, we are passing an order in a most peculiar logical form: "Do something which one will be inclined to accept as a solution even though one does not know what it will be like." We want to play chess even though we do not understand the role of the queen. Superlatives like the "general-will," the "sovereign," or the "state" cannot help us (nor can that omniscient spectator in modern dress, the "political system." These forms of expression indicate the failure of our forms of thought. They are like "pontificals" which we put on, perhaps, but with which we cannot do much since we lack the procedures to give them "meaning and purpose."

It is the function of political *thinking* — as opposed to the exposition of the history of political *thought* — to clarify, to undo, the entangled language of our discipline. Perhaps this clarification will reduce us to silence. One cannot be sure. But if silence is cowardice in the tragedy of political life, it is a kind of courage in the tragedy of political thought.

Brotherly Interlude IV

After Kafka, it was Georges Sorel to whom Jerry devoted most of his scholarly energies. Although a respectable body of literature had appeared on Sorel, it could hardly have been compared with the intellectual cottage industry that grew up around Kafka. Jerry's deep concern in the early 1960s with the issues raised by Sorel's writings — which would be revived by Marxists and others after the social turbulence of the late years of the decade and early 1970s — once again showed he was on the cutting edge of political thought. Sorel's contribution had previously been obscured by those analysts who relegated him merely to the position of precursor of fascism or as theorist of modern terrorism. Even Herbert Marcuse — whose departure from Brandeis in 1965 left a theoretical gap filled in part by Jerry — stated a direct connection between Sorel's concepts and the fascist programs. Sorel's awkward relationship with Marxism has also sown the seeds of confusion among social scientists. Sympathizers with Sorel tended to reduce his conception of violence to any form of revolutionary action that served to undermine the existing social order. Jerry, however, always focused on the texts, read Sorel's attempt to clarify the proletarian development of its revolutionary capacity as central to the building of communal solidarity and made it the cornerstone of his own conceptual approach to violence. Perhaps he saw a distinct parallel between Sorel's proletarian myth of the general strike and Black Muslim separatist ideology, with the white world substituting for Sorel's bourgeoisie. What forges unity of both the workers in Sorel's program and of the blacks in the Muslim program is their shared myth of violence that organizes them in constituting them as self-conscious groups willing in the abstract to engage in combat with the (white) capitalist ruling class.

The following essay was actually his dissertation prospectus submitted to his advisor Hannah Arendt, who wrote a postcard in hasty response declaring it "excellent" and desiring to see more. Here we see in the year of the Gulf of Tonkin resolution the first installment of Jerry's mature thought on the centrality of violence in the formation of the community. It is Sorel who first enunciated the idea that the authentic community emerges in the midst of combat, on the field of honor. Sorel also helped clarify Jerry's key theoretical notions that the risk of violent death constitutes society, and that the indivisible community is won mainly through the struggle of class divisions.

Violence and Myth: A Study of Georges Sorel

(1964)

Violence: The Duel with Political Philosophy

Sorel presumes to challenge the objective of the whole tradition of western political thought: the achievement of a higher or lower order of *civil* society. He believes the project of political philosophy is deranged by its very aim, deranged precisely because it is a *civil* philosophy; that is to say, it assumes the community is located in the affairs of the city. Sorel asserts, on the contrary, that true community emerges only in the midst of combat, on the field of honor. Therefore, the first and last depiction of community appears not in the *Republic*, but in the *Iliad*. The author of that book perceived that worthy men "were more enamoured with the thought of fighting than with their own country." The civil philosophy turned away from this standard. Indeed, the history of political thought can be viewed as the chronicle of escape from the Homeric community.

The escape has been made in two different directions, by two conventional, but divergent routes that are constituted finally as opposed schools of thought:
  1) The Moralists
  2) The Rationalists

Sorel believes that both of these otherwise incompatible approaches share a common standpoint, the standpoint of civil authority. Both express, according to our author, the civil order's underlying dread (*sous-terreur*) of free or indeterminate violence.

A) The Moralists, on the one hand, shun this frightening consideration by attaching obnoxious connotations to its manifestations: the act of violence is rejected either as an unqualified evil or justified, at best, as a last resort, as an exigency of individual or corporate self-defense.

B) The Rationalists, on the other hand, while freeing violence from its moral isolation, assume its value can only be measured by its predicted *consequences*. "If the [act of violence] *accuses* him, the results should excuse him (Machiavelli, *The Discourses*, Book 1, Ch. 9).

Sorel believes that both of these standpoints obscure the question of violence. He argues that the moralists are fundamentally occupied with assuaging middle-class fears of violence by perpetuating the middle-class illusion that violence only emanates from the remote margins of society: from the criminal and secret political societies, or, as we would say, from the underworld. By confining the problem to these sources, they conceal the possibility of the general outbreak of violence within civil society itself.

The rationalists beg the question by equating the tortured and unpredictable *process* of violence with the computed weight of the means of violence, i.e., established force. The "little science," as he calls it, assimilates the awful problem of violence to the routine processes of production and organization appropriate only to the *vie quotidienne* of civil society. Sorel suggests that the "little science" is terrified by the unaccountable, and, hence, gains an illusory comfort from futile computation.

Thus, while the Moralists and Rationalists approach violence form different directions, they are as one in their exclusion of the question from the civil world of conventional morality and conventional science.

Sorel aims to extricate the question from these veiled contexts and throw it into sharp relief. He wants to understand violence as a "pure" activity, as an autonomous process that cuts through the very foundation of the civil order. This understanding leads him, on the one hand, to the inversion of the conventional relation of morality to violence (the subject of Chapter II),1 and to the subversion of scientific explanations of violence on the other (the subject of Chapter III).

The relation of violence to community is not marginal for Sorel; its "regime," as he calls it, is at the very center of society. Its clients are neither outlaws on the one side, nor the segregated warrior-caste on the other. They are constituted, in fact, by the disinherited "army of battle that society carries *within* itself" — the proletariat.

Thus Sorel intends to draw the question out "from the shadows" of the underworld and away from the isolated camps of the professional warriors, and into the "broad daylight" of quotidian life. The source of violence can be openly viewed along the broad base of society, that is, in the working class. It is the violence at that base that concerns Sorel and provides the primary subject of his life's work. In assigning the revolutionary task to the proletarian majority, he, as we shall see, *generalizes* and *exalts* the role of violence.

Sorel inverts the role of violence *within* civil society, for he believes that it is the only means by which true community, i.e., fellowship, can be achieved. *Indivisible community is won only through class division.* (Here we must note that Sorel is not primarily concerned with war in its *foreign*, but in its *civil*, context. This emphasis will be marked throughout this study).

This community, conceived in its relation to the proletariat, emerges in the process of the *general strike*. For it is only through the general strike that the community, according to our author, "asserts its existence." The otherwise intimidated and atomized working class constitutes a community only when it undertakes the fight, and remains one only during combat, in the face of common disaster, in the fellowship of common sacrifice.[2]

Thus, the general strike cannot be confused with the "mercenary" *economic* strike. Transient and passive work-stoppage only reinforces the servility of the demoralized unions. The members view the strike only as a melancholy pause in the otherwise eternal humiliation that constitutes their way of life. But, by contrast, the general strike is not something peripheral or temporary in the life of the worker. Indeed, it is his *raison d'être*. In the corporate act of violence the servile producer is replaced by the liberated warrior. The bestial laborer experiences human freedom — otherwise a vacuous ideal — only by risking his life in the general strike. The compromised, mercenary, and craven life of quotidian values is suddenly and irrevocably abandoned in the collective ecstasy of "epic-consciousness."

It is at this point we may note Sorel's critical departure from Marx's theory of revolution. The French writer conceives of the heightened enthusiasm of the proletarian strike as free of any *calculation* of a future society of material favors or distributed largesse, i.e., "the classless society." *For it is just this form of bourgeois thinking that the heroic consciousness of the general strike is called upon to extinguish.* In the fervor of "epic-consciousness" the question of a future state is devoid of meaning. The heroic community enters a "pure duration" (Bergson), a "timeless time" that marks all states of moral sublimity. Time past and time future interpenetrate in the "continuous present," in the primordial release of the general strike.

Any selfish promptings of philosophic or material calculation can only depress the enthusiasm for the common sacrifice. The contemplation of abstract and remote utopias can only inhibit the outbreak of spontaneous and general violence. Thus Sorel addresses himself to Marx's utopia in no uncertain terms: "A man who draws up a program for the future is a reactionary." The heroic *myth* alone can unleash revolutionary violence; the mercenary's utopia can only inhibit it.

Now the myth as a spontaneous vision of pure battle images is only "a means of acting on the present" and survives only for the duration of combat. As the revolution runs its course, the collective ecstasy wanes, and the community of heroes falls away. When the object is attained, that is, when the destruction of Bourgeois society is completed, the *raison d'être* of the *general strike* passes away with it. The revolutionary community, like the Homeric community, *dissolves precisely as it reaches its goal*. The true community is bound by its purpose to an ephemeral life: a brief but fatal celebration. Its existence only survives as a legend in the collective memory of the subsequent generation. This we take to be the peculiar, if not paradoxical, substance of Sorel's "political" philosophy. The *community* emerges, for a moment, in the ruins of the *polity*.

Hobbes, it will be recalled, believed that civil society constituted an enduring, if ignoble refuge from the *fear* of violent death. For that very reason Sorel believed that civil society deserved to be destroyed: the noble, if brief community is constituted only through the risk of violent death.

VIOLENCE: FROM MORALITY TO MORALE

Violence can be understood, in Sorel's sense, as the extinction of social action. It represents the extinction of relationship on *contact*: "There where someone stood a moment ago, stands no one." The warrior engages his enemy to terminate all future engagements with him.

Yet this brief meeting is at the same time the most significant meeting of a lifetime: the lasting ties, the enduring love, the long, complex history of a man is ingathered at one point — and suddenly risked in an encounter with a stranger.[4] But this appears uncanny. Indeed, the longer one "reflects" on the question of violence from the framework of ordinary non-violent social processes, the more extraordinary, the more unbelievable the outbreak appears. But this incredulity only reveals the bias of our habitual modes of perception, and the overriding influence of our protected institutional standpoint. Perhaps this is why Sorel believed that no professional teacher could sensibly discuss the problem of violence. Awesome questions cannot be incorporated into traditional institutions.

Violence, in Sorel's sense, differs decisively from the sociological understanding of conflict or quarrel (in Simmel's sense of *Der Streit*); for the latter presupposes a continuous relationship which endures precisely because the mutual security of the participants (married couples, intimate friends, sporting rivals) is not threatened by the free and unreserved expression of hostility. In these relations, crises are less likely to be fatal challenges to the foundations. "The strongest love can take the severest blows most easily." Marriage, viewed from this perspective, is the freedom to express and the willingness to endure a conflict. In sum, if violence terminates, conflict sustains social action.

The violent act is not, in Sorel's terms, significant for its consequences. The distinction between victory and defeat is transient. The warrior is bound, by his vocation, to suffer both. Odysseus knows he is "duty bound to stand unflinchingly and to *kill* or *die*." But fortune, not man, marks the distinction. The consequences of the battle are unknown to the participants at the outset, but that is not the consideration; for it is the *willingness* to face the unknown that constitutes, in the last analysis, the vocation of the warrior. What is significant, then, is not the outcome of the engagement, but the willingness of the combatants to confront the immediate possibility of death. This willingness includes deliberate martyrdom, as well as open combat. For Sorel, the martyr *attacks his enemy* by destroying his own *body*. It is, for that reason, no less heroic than the fight. Thus, our author wants to understand violence, not in terms of consequences, but in terms of will — destructive will.

Here Sorel ranges himself alongside Schopenhauer (but draws a radically different conclusion), and against Rousseau and Kant. Will is not constitutive or constructive; it is *pure* destruction. According to Sorel, a man can achieve a state of moral sublimity only in willing-to-violence, only when he is prepared to sacrifice his life. Thus, Sorel not only asserts that a) morality cannot exist apart from the act of violence, but that b) readiness for violence *induces* moral sensibility.

Thus, Sorel claims that Christianity cannot be understood by way of the Gospels (unmemorable in themselves), but only through an appreciation of the martyrdoms that preceded and succeeded the transcription of the teaching. The religious, as opposed to philosophical-significance of Socrates resides not in his discourse, but in his unnatural (edifying) death. By the same token one can understand *l'éthique vivante* of socialism, not by reading Fourier, but by visualizing the general strike.

The sacred departs from the secular only, in other words, through the medium of violence. Indeed, the *sacred* not only shares its meaning, but owes its life to the blood *sacrifice*. In his work on Renan's histories, Sorel declares that violence is the "aphrodisiac" of virtue. It is not accidental that the denouement of the *Réflexions*, the seventh chapter, is entitled *La moralité de la violence*.

The significance of this radical upturning of the "conventional" relation between morality and violence can be seen by contrast with the position of St. Augustine. The latter identifies violence with the waywardness of the secular realm. Even the "just war" he holds to be a "cruel necessity" and, in any case, characteristic of that city founded by a fratricide. (See the *City of God* XV, 5; XIX, 7.)

Sorel's "transvaluation" appears less shocking, however, if one notes the special connotation he attaches to the term. Morality, according to Sorel, is the state of "epic-consciousness" won only on the field of honor. Only battle can evoke man's "noblest" and most "serious" instincts. Moral sublimity is the condition of the hero at the moment of attack. It corresponds to the ecstatic abandonment of all the "civic virtues," worldly loves, and material profits. Only in *battle* can one find true ascetics. Sorel goes so far as to deny the moral value of any religious conduct based on quotidian standards. This includes the monastic vocation of *routine* asceticism, e.g., the Benedictine rule of work and worship.

Thus, we can understand the morality of epic-consciousness by that term introduced in the exalted days of the French Revolution — *morale*.

Morale broadens the meaning of heroism. It cannot be restricted to the romantic, detached figure exalted, for instance, in Carlyle's work. For a movement that requires the recruitment of the great body of the working class, the supreme act of virtuosity has meaning only as a point of *inspiration* for the body of uncertain volunteers. The splendid deeds of Achilles and Patroclus have significance only as they are reflected in the rejuvenated morale of their fellow Achaeans. Morale, then, is the irresistible conduction of epic-consciousness *through the ranks*, by exemplary acts of violence.

Sorel distinguishes the heroic violence of combat from the "illicit" uses of violence within the institutional structure of civil society. These uses represent a *profanation of violence*, if violence is conceived as the pure and unadulterated expression of will, called up in the gallant moment of combat.

These profane uses of civil violence are

1) Police or custodial force, and, on the other hand,

2) Criminal violence (homicide and brigandage).

Profane forms of violence are "illicit," according to Sorel (after Proudhon), because they conceal and pervert its "pure" expression. The custodians of force, on the one hand, self-righteously conceal their *motives* in executing the victim. The morbid "triumphs" of capital punishment cloak, in fact, the obscene desires of a bourgeois public, *demoralized* by its fear of open and honorable combat. (If *morale* is the exalted virtue of the proletarian warriors, *demoralization*, characterized as the middle-class fear of violence, represents, in Sorel's code, the ultimate vice.) The prudent and timorous middle-class expresses its moral decadence in the vicarious torture and execution of an already defenseless captive.

The criminal, on the other hand, undertakes his act in secret, for the sake of winning sudden riches, and thus demonstrates, at the extreme, the "lunacy" of bourgeois aspiration.

Violence as "pure" will is, thus, profaned and adulterated, in the first use, by the perverse concealment of the *motives* governing the use of custodial force; and in the second, by the perfidious concealment of the *act* of violence. The police power conceals its *motives*, and the criminal hides his *acts*. (Sorel, it should be said, expresses sympathy for the uncorrupted and candid *crime of passion*, even though it lacks the heroic attribute that hallows the *willing* sacrifice of corporate combat.)

The profane violence committed within the interstices of the bourgeois order reveals the deep-going crisis of its way of life. It is the task of the anointed proletariat to purify the unsalvageable decadence of modern society, not by awaiting, but by initiating the apocalypse.

THE "NECESSITY" OF FORCE AND THE AUTONOMY OF VIOLENCE

Sorel equates the eruption of violence in society with the emergence of Bergson's élan vital in the natural world.[5] As life for Bergson is an explosive liberation from the prison of the inert material world, so the outbreak of violence liberates the human will from the tyranny of decaying civil order. Indeed, Sorel insists that Bergson's *élan* is more appropriately placed in social dynamics than in biology. Bergson himself, he says, is disposed to study non-human phenomena from the standpoint of the human, thus reversing Darwin's treatment of evolution. It is worth noting in support of Sorel here, that Bergson adopts a remarkable number of metaphors taken over from the military sciences to his biological thesis. At various points in his *Essai* and *Evolution créatrice* he compares life to a cavalry charge, cannon shells exploding into fragments, *ad infinitum*, a coup d'état of the mind, waves overcoming fortresses, etc. The key metaphor for life, according to Bergson's usage, is an *explosion*.

Sorel claims that a violent act is an extraordinary assertion of the will that cannot be explained by the motives of everyday conduct. We remember that Bergson had argued that will, at "a great and solemn crisis, can choose in defiance of what is conventionally called a motive, and this absence of any tangible reason is the more striking the deeper our freedom goes." Thus, neither the outbreak nor the consequences of revolutionary violence can be predicted or accounted for by a social science based on an assumption of a violence-free routine of daily conduct.

The sophistries of the "little science" consist precisely in putting very different things on the same plane; the question of violence, however, can no more be reduced to the number and scale of fire-arms in society than sexual conduct can be reduced to the umber of marriage contracts delivered each year. But it is the business of middle-class science, he says, to treat dangerous things as if they were routine. The scientists are obliged to bring about the disappearance of unpleasant facts that plague their capitalist directors. Middle-class science is a "mill" that produces solutions to the problems faced by the bourgeoisie. The social scientists are therefore disposed to explain away or avoid the unknown factors, the insoluble difficulties that confront the men they serve, for they fear the consequences of frightening their masters. Sorel proposes, therefore, to reveal the barrenness of these scientific solutions by directing the reader's attention to the indeterminate regions, i.e., the "regime of violence" which the "little science" abhors.

Sorel's application of Bergson's metaphysics of indeterminism allows him to make a distinction between a) the *force* of established authority and b) the unassayable regime of *violence*. The aim of the established institution of force is to mechanize obedience, to produce servility in the working class on the same level of efficiency that the working class produces commodities. The mode of production is the model of domination.

All of bourgeois invention and progress resulted, as Marx said, "in endowing material forces with intellectual life, and in stultifying human life into a material force." Sorel believed, with Marx, that the system that degraded spontaneous and free human activity into a means was bound for a violent end; but he radically opposed, as we shall see, Marx's "mechanistic subjection" of revolutionary violence.

In the process of reducing men to means, says Sorel, the bourgeoisie bind the question of violence out of their world-view: their fear of its outbreak is counteracted by the reassurance they receive from observing the productive regimen, day in and day out. Thus, the bourgeoisie, as a matter of habit, do not make a human, but only an economic distinction between the inert and living means of production.

This fatal habit of the entrepreneur is born of his own *competence*. Deceived by the efficient routinization of the administrative and productive processes which he commands, he assumes he can automatize obedience as he mechanized production. By constitution, he overlooks or isolates those developments that cannot be assimilated to his rational economy of means, and, as Sorel suggests, avoids coming to grips with those dangerous and unaccountable "springs of life ever forcing their way to the surface."[6]

Human performance, on Sorel's account, cannot be subjected to a predetermined regimen; for in its decisive moments, unique and unrepeatable, the human will breaks from its fixed course and cannot be recalled to its former position. It is no accident that the onset of insurrection appears "unbelievable" or "miraculous" to the established authorities, for this outbreak is tantamount, on their view, to an extraordinary interruption in the recurrent processes of nature. But the outbreak of revolutionary violence gives the lie to the illusion that social power, i.e., force, cannot be conserved like kinetic energy. Bourgeois society collapses because it cannot *enforce its illusion of force*, and bourgeois science falls with it because its mode of explanation and prediction is based on the very same ideological presupposition. Sorel, thus, identifies force with the illusion of necessity, and violence with the assertion of freedom.

Taken from the other side of the bourgeois nexus of production, Sorel admits that the laborer remains indistinguishable from the *instrumentum mutum* unless and until he liquidates the reductionist forces of capital. So long as the proletarian simulates the *perpetuum mobile* of the "industrial planet" and accepts his segmented function within it, he cannot discern his special relationship to the industrial environment. But, to establish this differentiation, the worker must win more than class-consciousness, he must abstract himself, quite exceptionally, from the working condition altogether.

Therefore, when the proletariat revolt they are not only emancipated from a certain relation to the means of production; they perceive in the same moment, the generic condition of their humanity. If we understand Sorel rightly, he is, then, saying something quite remarkable and, what is more, something in flagrant opposition to the founder of Scientific Socialism. For Sorel, unlike Marx, the central question is not whether the laborer must either "employ the means of production" or be "employed by the means of production" (*Capital*, Ch. XI), but, on the contrary, the problem is to discover an autonomous position in the communal process completely outside the productive process — whatever its social form.

In light of what we have already seen, this position presupposes the *autonomy of violence*, for that condition alone is coeval with the circumstance of unintimidated freedom. As against revolutionary action, *work is ministerial*, and involves, as a species of behavior, however one divides it, "mechanical and servile routine."

Sorel's conception of the general strike entails, perforce, not only a transposition of the capitalist's *animal laborans*, but a subversion, as well, of Marx's *homo faber*; for against both he asserts the primacy of *homo violentus*.

Thus Sorel's critique of bourgeois determinism, oriented by Bergson's radical metaphysics, led him ineluctably to challenge, not without embarrassment, Marx's dialectical materialism; for Marx was no less deterministic than the "little science" in his treatment of social change. Moreover, the venerated master's theory of violence was assimilated to that determinism. Sorel is forced to conclude, with uncharacteristic reluctance, that Marx was infected with bourgeois scientific notions.

Marx had compared violence with a midwife. But a midwife, after all, must await a determinate period of gestation before she can assist the birth of the offspring, i.e., unleash the revolution. Here Marx provides mechanistic explanation to the eruption of violence — an explanation absolutely unacceptable to Sorel.

Furthermore, Marx had anticipated the cessation of violence at a "final" historical stage; he foresaw its elimination in a "classless society." In this way, Marx's mechanism assumes that the future remains implicit in the past, for it affirms that the end to be achieved can be known in advance; and it denies the possibility of a novel outcome to historical process. This denial supposes the disappearance of the action of autonomous will at some point in the future. But for Sorel, on the contrary, the repeated outbreak of violence proved again and again that no society could achieve ultimate stability — whatever its mode of production and distribution.

"We don't believe in the fatality of history; there is no obstacle that cannot be broken down by wills sufficiently keyed up, if they deal with it in time.... There is no inescapable historical law."[7] The social process, according to Sorel, has no end-point. It is unceasing novelty. It is a shell exploding into fragments, those fragments, in turn, exploding into other fragments, *ad infinitum*. Bergson's metaphysics of indeterminism is invoked against Marx's scientific socialism. "The passage from capitalism to socialism must be conceived as a catastrophe, the development of which baffles description." Nor is socialism, in its turn, vouchsafed from the catastrophic, but rejuvenating explosion of heroic will. Thus, if violence was, for Marx, the midwife of history, history, for Sorel, is the midwife to violence.

Sorel's differentiation of force and violence leads us to consider a distinction that is only implicit in his work, but which, I believe, requires articulation: the distinction between the *means* of violence and the *process* of violence. Since Weber, the latter has often been uncritically assimilated to the former. The collapse of this distinction we call an instrumental bias, for it reduces the problem of violence to the problem of *inventory*: if one wishes to understand the nature of violence, one needs but consider the number and variety of "tools," i.e., weapons, and their mode of deployment by the "specialists of violence" (Lasswell). But clearly, this begs the question, for the possession of a revolver is not yet the *critical use* of a weapon. The use has consequences not foreseen in mere possession and know-how. The point is that the "tools" in the armory are neither tools in the conventional sense of the word, nor is the warrior unambiguously an "artisan." He does not make tables or chairs; nor does he fashion artifacts. His tools are not designed for construction, but destruction — destruction of human life.[8] (Could one possibly say *the warrior uses his tools to construct a death*?) The *end* of this artisan's work is not a creation, but an annihilation. But, however inadvertently, modern political scientists and sociologists are prone, almost without exception, to confound the civil *means of production* with fatal *means of violence*. Marx was well aware of this danger, and reminded his readers that the professional "military people" are "not only not productive, but essentially destructive" (*Theories of Surplus Value*, p. 175).

The violent engagement precipitates the most unpredictable consequences in the human environment and this extremity can only intensify the desperation and disarray produced in the area of combat. War is, after all, a process of continuous *deformation* of the human and physical environment. The longer the fight continues, the less reliable appear those judgments formed at the outbreak of the struggle. The unexpected and tortured outcome of warfare only demonstrates the utter vanity of reducing the question of the indeterminate process to the determinate means of violence.

The instrumental bias assumes that the consequences of unleashing the means can be determined at the moment one has concluded an account of the production, organization and deployment of those means. The "little science" is consumed with the spirit of *geometry*, as Bergson would say, when it requires the spirit of *finesse*.

THE INTERPENETRATION OF MYTH AND VIOLENCE

In bourgeois society, Sorel asserts, the measured relation between thought and action constitutes an essential *duplicity*. Thought begins with concealment and, following the inevitable delay of calculation, ends in deceptive action. Thus, thinking is identified with a private, i.e., hidden process. Men are careful not to think "out loud" for fear of exposing their mercenary intentions and, in public, candor is generally taken for a form of madness. If men are to successfully compete with, and exploit their fellows, they must not reveal their calculations — the mind must be treated as a vault. Taken from the standpoint of the *other*, actions appear as maneuvers that cannot be easily understood because they dissimulate, often as not, the hidden intent of the action.

The Cartesian dualism (mind-body) can be conceived as a philosophic elaboration of mercantile duplicity. This duplicity is the prime target of our author's critique of bourgeois decadence.

The two strategic terms in Sorel's partisan dictionary are *violence* and *myth*. We have noticed that violence appears in Sorel's revolutionary drama as the extinction of secular action, and we shall see that myth correspondingly appears as the suspension of critical thought. But we would be mistaken if we conceived of myth and violence as another dualism. On the contrary, they comprise an inseparable unity. The union emerges precisely in the attempt to overcome the irreducible *gap* between thinking and acting. Myth and violence are joined at the extremity of secular life in a single aspiration: the abolition of prudential, i.e., duplicitous conduct. Insofar as Sorel's commentators have treated myth and violence as separate questions, they have missed a decisive point in his work.

Sorel agrees with Renan that myth does not enclose two elements, an inside (private thought) and an outside (public act). Mythic possession is rather an undivided state of heightened adoration, "free of reflection and all premeditated subtlety." Epic-consciousness is a state of intense and undivided thralldom. The mythic image, e.g., "Delacroix's Liberty Leading the People," entirely fills the consciousness, and nothing else in the moment can exist apart from or beside it. The ego compresses all its energy on a single point, lives in it, loses itself in it. There is no duplicity in "epic-consciousness." It is a "one-possibility" thing.

In the modern world, where quotidian standards of utility have corrupted the rich sources of primordial enthusiasm, the only "pure" environment capable of "evoking images one can genuinely express without deception or self-deception" is the battlefield. "Men," Sorel says, "who participate in great social movements always picture their coming action as a *battle* in which their cause is certain to triumph. These images, I propose to call myths." Thus, the mythic intuition and the battle situation are interdependent. If one tries to analyze them separately, one is led back to their underlying unity.

This unity is perhaps best expressed by Sorel's notion of the "general strike." On first inspection, the expression appears confused by the attachment of two unresolved meanings. He alternately labels it a *myth*, and then again, an *act* of corporate violence. The strike signifies, on the one hand, the "myth in which socialism is wholly comprised," and on the other, the "Napoleonic Battle" or simply the "course of social war." But this confusion disappears if one understands the general strike as a body of images capable of evoking the instinctive "sentiments of violence" otherwise dormant in the proletariat. One is freed from the world *symbolically* as one engages to destroy it in *fact*.

This symbolic freedom is effected, in the world of "pure duration" (Bergson); or, in more recent terms, "a time out of time" (Stanner), or the "continuous present" (Eliade). The participants, in Sorel's case, enter this state through the medium of "sacred fury." Like the frenzied *Beserkirs*, the modern proletariat, possessed of the *élan révolutionnaire fébrile*, are carried over the barricades — out of this world.

The myth considered in its relation to its subjects is properly called an image, and not a representation. In the subjective attitude of epic-consciousness, the warrior no longer accounts for the material obstacles in his path, nor does he record the objective passing of time. Indeed, as we have seen, there is no experience of time in the conventional (chronological) sense of the word. In the duration of the strike, images of struggles in the antique past fuse with the vision of the immediate combat. Sorel suggests that the aspect under which the combatants experience war corresponds to the "tone" set by the Homeric battles. Every heroic deed recapitulates, in the moment, the primordial ancestry of the deed.

Representations, on the other hand, are worked up through reflection, and are characteristically theoretic and objective. They denote, or ultimately refer to, objects in space and dated events in time. These representations elaborate and attenuate spontaneous expression, and subdivide the "momentary deity" into graduated and measurable units of time. In Bergson's terms, the image *endures*, the representation *succeeds*.

When these representations are worked out systematically and propagated through the social structure, they are called *utopias*. Sorel does not differentiate these intellectual constructions as does Mannheim, for example. Utopian orientations, whether they defend the *status quo* (liberal democracy) or challenge it (Fourier's "phalanstery," Marx's "classless society"), are, in the most decisive respects, one and the same: They inhibit violent action.

The inhibitions of bourgeois liberalism operate through the borrower's ideal of "progress." Aside from its philosophical-historical significance, this deal reduces to the proposition: riches may be gained on the morrow if present liabilities are sustained. Or, as Keynes was to later phrase it: "a case of jam tomorrow, and never jam today." In a world of credit no one ever acts entirely in the present. Thus, the rational economy of time dissipates the motive force of all great deeds. The obsession with the clock and the schedule enslaves the bourgeoisie, for they cannot escape time.

On the other hand, the Utopias that reject the *status quo* also abort spontaneous action, for their intellectual dreams appear too remote to inspire violence in the present. When men read Saint-Simon and Fourier, they don't act, they dream; but this dream is only the other side of that private world of mercenary calculation — on its day off. The romantic dreams of the philosophers enter the salons, but never the militant world of direct action. These isolated daydreams represent, at best, an innocuous respite from the intolerable duplicity of bourgeois conduct.

Thus "ideologies" and "utopias" come to the same thing: the eternal postponement of decisive, that is violent action.

The Utopia of bourgeois "progress" inhibits direct action, for its paradisiacal tomorrow appears so *near*. The Utopia of the philosophers depresses revolutionary fervor, for their tomorrow is so utterly *remote*.

Not philosophy, but the myth alone can inspire the revolutionary act and "free" the proletariat from the mundane world.[9] The craven and petty duplicity of quotidian thought and action is finally consumed in the primordial enthusiasm and visionary prospect of the general strike.

THE GENERAL WILL TRANSFORMED: THE GENERAL STRIKE

Sorel believes, as we have seen, that the community can assert itself not through the integration, but only through the division of society. The community of authentic fellowship, free of all civil duplicity, surfaces only in the process of the general strike, e.g., in the cleavage of "social war."

Community cannot be achieved, on the other hand, in a state of civil peace, for the "pacifist ideal is grafted on the degeneration of the capitalist system," a system that degrades all sentiments of honor (the military virtue) — the only basis of true and open fellowship. Bourgeois society undermines and compromises all honorable differences, and cowardly aborts the only mode of honorable settlement (trial by combat). It confines all "disputes, instead, around material interests, where there is no more opportunity for heroism than can be found in the negotiations of the agricultural syndicates settling the price of guano with manure merchants."

Sorel's understanding of revolutionary community is not unrelated to his frequent assaults on Rousseau's *Social Contract*. In that work, Jean-Jacques visualized civil society redeemed by the formal achievement of the *general will*. The latter can be expressed only after man has learned to "consult his reason" and ceased "listening to his inclinations." Through the founding act, "man loses his natural liberty, and an unlimited right to all which tempts him; in return he acquires *civil* liberty." Thus the natural will of the solitary, pre-civil man is universalized by reason and expressed collectively as the general will.

Sorel's understanding of the *will* directly opposes Rousseau's "abstract construction." Corporate willing, for our author, can neither be 1) rational, nor 2) constitutive; but is expressed, rather, through the linked relation of myth and violence.

Sorel tells us that community can only be based on myth; not *logos*, but *mythos* corresponds to the corporate consciousness of the community. Indeed, discursive reason accentuates self-consciousness and, hence, alienation from community. Only in the undivided state of epic-consciousness, in the act of heroic self-abandonment, can people experience primordial communion. Thus, the indivisible communion is created in the myth of the general strike, not in the reason of the general will.

Let us recall that the mythic consciousness that is awakened in the general strike is not prompted by calculation, or as Rousseau would say, "deliberation." All such rational-economic models of thought are precisely what the myth of the general strike is called upon to eliminate. Any calculation made with an eye toward the future benefits reintroduces, at once, mercenary self-interest in the very act of founding. The general will dissolves precisely when deliberation begins. That is why we can only visualize the *Social Contract* in its moment of initiation. It can never get over its own beginning. It is a machine that flies apart precisely when it begins to move.

All such deliberations are displaced in the corporate morale of the general strike; the cold calculations of reason give way to the most "uneconomical," that is, dangerous of human expressions — spontaneous ardor. This ardor is identical with the primitive convictions of the group and "cannot be elaborated by discursive means." The *corporate intuition*, which the slow inventory of reason can only dissipate, is obtained "as a whole, and perceived instantaneously." The achievement of "epic-consciousness" forbids any objective conception of society.[10] It is the myth in its entirety and indivisibility which is alone important. Thus, the myth of the general strike, treated from the standpoint of ", overcomes the gap between society and the individual; as epic- consciousness, viewed from the standpoint of the individual, transcends the intolerable duplicity of thought and action.

Now we may approach the second, but immediately related point of opposition between Rousseau and Sorel. The latter assumed that unanimity of society was constituted by the elimination of division. He had written: "It is of the utmost importance for the expression of the general will that no partial society should be formed in the state." Indeed, "there is no longer a general will when one of the partial associations is so great that it carries the others along." When there are no longer as many individual votes as men, but only as many as there are associations, the union dissolves.

Sorel, on the other hand, denies, as we have seen, that indivisible will can be constituted by atomic individuals in the civil void. The community can achieve unity only through common sacrifice. The community is created where Rousseau's general will breaks down in faction or, in Sorel's favored expression, *scission*. The corporate will is only expressed in heroic *revolt* against the civil order — in spite of all material obstacles, and against all better judgment. The indivisible morale of community requires the division of demoralized society. Pure will, therefore, is manifest in the primordial act of destruction, and not in the civil act of construction.

The ethical and political unity of the antique city (most especially Sparta) that inspired Rousseau is recaptured in the modern world, not through the instrument of the mercenary bargain, i.e., *contract*, but through the common self-sacrifice of the general strike. Indeed, after the Commune of 1871 the disinherited no longer were to call up the dream of bourgeois reason — the general will; but invoked, in its place, the myth of the proletarian general strike.

But the community only endures as long as it sustains morale, and morale is bound to disappear when the task of the revolution is completed. Sorel was aware that the community of civil warriors was, at best, a momentary phenomenon ("five minutes of direct action is worth twenty years of parliamentary chatter"), for the heightened enthusiasm of epic-consciousness could not be sustained indefinitely. The heroes fall away as destruction runs its course. When the civil order is crushed, the *raison d'être* of the revolutionary commune is lost. If, on the other hand, the revolution is defeated by the established forces, the general strike survives only in the underground memory of the subsequent generation. The revolutionary community passes away, whether it fails or succeeds. The true community, like the hero himself, exists only for a season. For the community, like Achilles, has "death for a future, the future assigned by the profession."

Something more than Sorel's antipathy to the traditional civil values of political theory and his unreserved affection for the war goddess disorients the reader: it is the temporal dimension implicit in his approach. This approach radically disorients our inveterate spatial mode of apprehending the community, and challenges our understanding of it as a fixed geographical location on a map, constituted by a stable-base population. But, with Sorel, we are disposed to face a *temporal community* — a community that asserts its existence at no predetermined point in space, but emerges in a wide variety of places; perhaps only for a brief duration, perhaps periodically — in any case, a community characteristically transient. This might lead us to examine the whole question of what could be called: the social structure of time.

CONCLUSION

VIOLENCE: THE END OF REFLECTION

Here we ask: can anything significant be said, indeed, can we "reflect" at all on the question of violence?

NOTES

The body of Sorel's published work appeared initially as articles in a wide variety of French, German and Italian journals. Most of these pieces were later collected in twelve books: *Contribution à l'étude profane de la Bible* (1889); *Le Procès de Socrate* (1889); *La Ruine du monde antique* (1898); *Introduction à l'économie moderne* (1903); *Le Système historique de Renan* (1906); *La Décomposition du Marxisme* (1908); *Réflexions sur la violence* (1908); *Les illusions du progrès* (1908); *La Révolution dreyfusienne* (1909); *Matériaux d'une théorie du prolétariat* (1919); *De l'utilité du pragmatisme* (1921); *D'Aristotle à Marx* (1935). At the time of Jerry's writing, only two works had been translated into English: *Réflexions on Violence* (translated by T. E. Hulme), and *The Decomposition of Marxism* (translated by I. L. Horowitz). Almost all of Sorel's work has been collected at the Bibliothèque Nationale, where the research on this study was completed.

1. It will be noticed that Sorel's inversion of the conventional relation between morality and violence corresponds closely to Nietzsche's "transvaluation of all values." Indeed, both deify, in Nietzsche's terms, "splendid animalism" and the "instincts of war," and both, on the other hand, degrade the "servile" and "hair-splitting" morality of civil life. It would seem more than a remarkable coincidence if it were not so utterly consistent that both Nietzsche and Sorel should launch their careers by attacking the "serpent" Socrates who separated western man from

primordial bliss by seducing him to eat of the withering tree of knowledge — that is, the tree of shame. Both, therefore, direct their initial works (*The Birth of Tragedy*, 1871; *The Trial of Socrates*, 1889) against the attenuating culture of the occident by assailing the prime legislator of that culture. They intend first of all to exercise the demon who first of all corrupted the incorporate and unblemished energies of the Achaean hero. They must pull down Socrates, "that shadow eating off a shadow," if they are to reconstitute the integral man.

But if their radical critique of civil morality coincides, the bases of their "new" morality radically diverge. Nietzsche's new men are an aristocratic minority of "mighty men" whose mark of distinction is made manifest by their capacity to transcend "everything . . . that brings the 'people' or 'woman' to the front, that operates in favor of the dominion of 'inferior men'." The heroic "Will to Power" is but the noble legacy of the few.

Sorel, on the other hand, places the burden of resurrection on the backs of the "slaves of history," the working class. The vehicle of his apocalyptic hope, the general strike, is constituted by the revolutionary mass that Nietzsche had regarded as the "mediocre, ignoble vermin-men." Sorel, to the contrary, believed that the general strike could elevate the whole body of the working class to the heights of heroism. While men are consumed by the epic-consciousness of battle, they are raised to the peak of aristocratic *élan*. The strike, in other words, *generalizes* the heroism of the exceptional figure. Indeed, Sorel viewed the conception of the "lonely hero" as a dream of wounded bourgeois vanity. The contrast could not be more striking. Nietzsche says "the misfortunes of the small folks do not constitute a sum-total, except in the *feelings* of *mighty* men." Sorel asserts that the heroic act is meaningful only within the corporate *morale* of the revolutionary syndicate.

2. An unsurpassed portrait of the inspired community of warriors appears in a fifteenth century autobiographical romance, *Le Jouvencel*, by Jean de Bueil (quoted by Johan Huizinga):

> "It is a joyous thing, is war. . . . You love your comrade so in war. When you see that your quarrel is just and your blood is fighting well, tears rise to your eye. A great sweet feeling of loyalty and of pity fills your heart on seeing your friend so valiantly exposing his body to execute and accomplish the command of our Creator. And then you prepare to go and die or live with him, and for love not to abandon him. And out of that there arises such a delectation, that he who has not tasted it is not fit to say what a delight it is. Do you think that a man who does that fears death? Not at all; for he feels so strengthened, he is so elated, that he does not know where he is. Truly he is afraid of nothing."

3. Sorel continually confounds *bourgeois* society with *civil* society, and he appears, in the process, to be confusing certain historical "relations of production" with the venerable abstraction of jurisprudence and political philosophy. Sorel,

in fact, comprehends both these expressions in an even wider sense. Civil society represents the transformation of irreconcilable, i.e., honorable divisions between classes and individuals into non-violent, i.e., dishonorable, disputes negotiated by the exchange of economic values.

4. Sorel is only occupied with violence as direct contact between human agents. The modern means of mass annihilation, on the other hand, presuppose an ever widening distance between opposing force (conceived as a function of the delivery system), and an enormously expanded perimeter of destruction (conceived as a function of the payload). The human, i.e., heroic factor is consequently abstracted from the combat situation. Accordingly, the heroic identity and its concomitant responsibility is removed from the human actor and transferred, as it were, to the weapons- system itself. Therefore, we should not be surprised to discover the pathos of this transformation incorporated into the rocket nomenclature: Nike, Hercules, Ajax, Atlas, Titan, etc.

But this recourse to the epic models of war in the nuclear age, that is, the *apotheosis of the missile system*, reveals a harrowing paradox. The inveterate longing for contact combat in its classic guise is attached to the very technology that has reduced the heroic duel to absurdity. In spite of the prodigious losses suffered by the antagonists and their respective populations, they have, for all that, never faced their rivals, never, as Homer would have it, "approached each other's eyes in the clamour of battle," and, therefore, we have suffered what is, from the classic vantage, unendurable: disability *sans* combat. How odd, then, seems the celebrated Quixotism of our Secretary of State on the aftermath of the Cuban missile crisis: "When we were eye-ball to eye-ball, the other fellow blinked."

On the occasion of the climactic nuclear "showdown," on the contrary, the *justi hostes* remains, in unprecedented exception, an *unseen enemy*. Indeed, one does not fall in mortal combat with the honorable glimpse of even a solitary belligerent. For the *strategic* nuclear assault is not endured on the *militiae*, the field of honor, but is received passively and anonymously in the peaceful confines of home and neighborhood. What is anomalous then, from Sorel's standpoint, is that in the most violent war imaginable, i.e., the automatic exchange of nuclear rockets, there are no human engagements and, accordingly, no human combatants. Everyone dies a civil death in the most terrible of all wars.

5. In spite of Sorel's many philosophic and ideological tribulations, Bergson's influence on his work is continuous (and this in spite of recurring attacks of anti-semitism), and it is not surprising that his respect for Bergson, though sometimes begrudging, never wavered. He compares him with *"un arbre vigoureux qui s'élève au milieu des steppes désolées de la philosophie contemporaine."*

Nor did Bergson have a low opinion of him. In a letter to Gilbert Maire he wrote, *"Ce n'est pas un disciple mais il accepte quelques-unes des mesures et quand il me cite il le fait en homme qui m'a parfaitement compris."*

6. Cf. Marx, *Capital*, Chapter XV, section 3.b:.

"In the first place, in form of machinery, the implements of labour become automatic, things moving and working independent of the workman. . . . The automation, as capital, and because it is capital, is endowed, in the person of the capitalist, with intelligence and will; it is therefore animated by the longing to reduce to a minimum the resistance offered by that repellant yet elastic natural barrier, man."

7. Bergson writes in *Evolution créatrice*: *"Pour arriver au principe de toute vie comme aussi de toute matérialité, il faudrait aller plus loin encore. . . . Quand nous replaçons notre être dans notre vouloir. . . nous comprenons, nous sentons que la réalité est une croissance perpétuelle, une création qui se poursuit sans fin. Notre volonté fait déjà ce miracle. Toute oeuvre humaine qui renferme une part d'invention, tout acte volontaire qui renferme une part de la liberté, tout mouvement d'un organisme qui manifeste de la spontanéité apporte quelque chose de nouveau dans le monde."*

8. The tragic dimension of this point is perhaps best expressed by Simone Weil: "The warrior's death itself is his future, the future assigned to him by his profession."

9. Contrast this view with the dictum of Marx: "Philosophy cannot realize itself without abolishing the proletariat, and the proletariat cannot emancipate itself without *realizing philosophy.*"

10. To be sure, Sorel entertained Utopian ideas of his own and, over the years, was attracted to an incredible variety of what he would call "utopian" movements, including: Syndicalism (C.G.T.), *Action Française*, Bolshevism, and Fascism. Commentators have often noted the ideological inconsistencies in these itinerant shifts in loyalty, but clearly there is a set of fundamental attitudes revealed through the motley nature of these attachments:
    1)   An enduring hatred for the bourgeoisie
    2)   A commitment to direct action, i.e. violence — regardless of the ideological consequences.
It was almost a feature of his style to contemptuously dismiss the cooked-up ideas of these movements, but then go on to praise their *élan* .

BROTHERLY INTERLUDE V

The intersection of Jerry's study of Sorel with the onset of the Vietnam War and domestic insurrection sparked his intense investigation of the pervasive problem of violence in modern society. His teaching at Brandeis, as reflected in the research papers of his students, and his prodigious production of notes in the period 1968-1969, demonstrate the degree to which the original monographic emphasis on Sorel had dramatically shifted to a full-scale exploration of the central role of violence in the social structure. In a sense, Jerry's attempt to find order and pattern where formerly only the erratic and unpredictable had been observed paralleled the pioneering work of chaos scientists modeling systems of random and disorderly phenomena. At the same time, one can hardly fail to grasp the Foucauldian implications of Jerry's thesis that the bourgeois state encourages violence as an instrument for controlling and policing its populace. The following pages are based on his voluminous notes from late 1968 through June 1969, when he began systematizing his thoughts on the civil and fraternal forms of power. They reveal his relentless subjection of the concept of violence to thorough-going analysis from the ground floor up and may serve as an introduction to his mature formulation.

NOTES TOWARDS AN UNDERSTANDING OF VIOLENCE

(1969)

It would seem odd, if not altogether paradoxical, to ascribe a *structure* to violence. If anything, its outbreak is apprehended in terms to the precise contrary, conjuring up as it does the sudden ruin and baneful dissipation, the "building down" of all the arduously cultivated institutions raised by human intelligence, elaborated and refined by social custody and otherwise vouchsafed to posterity by venerable tradition.

No one would wish to deny, least of all myself, the awful contact the sweep of violence makes with our tense thought and deepest fears that renders the very mention of the word an occasion for calling out the reflexive imagery of chaos and dissolution. But when the problem is conceived in this way, implicitly or explicitly, we are dispossessed of the very ground of systematic investigation. For having already excommunicated the question to a "chaos of levity and ferocity," we lack what is indispensable to further scrutiny, namely, a set of relationships, however disorderly in appearance, that are sufficiently coherent in composition and continuous in sequence to provide the minimal requirement of theoretical analysis.

But this is precisely what is denied by the traditional orientation, so far as the process of violence is conceptually disintegrated in the forsworn terms of a boundless, arbitrary, and discontinuous void. Once it is assumed that the social condition cannot secure integrity "in any other state of things," as Burke resolves, beyond the inclusive sphere of civil society, than it must be concluded that as the magnitude of violent behavior increases at the locus of civil order, the intelligibility of social phenomena correspondingly decreases.

It is altogether unsurprising that the traditions controlling the discussion of violence, having previously denied its structural coherence, generate, as a last ascriptive resort, vacuous epithets for want of explanation, e.gs., "gratuitous, "senseless," "unnatural," "irrational," "fortuitous, "pathological," and so on. In fact, in our common currency, the term violent appears as a veritable synonym for the incomprehensible. What uncontrollably frightens us in the deed is removed from direct and unencumbered considerations in thought. The civil imperative generates and becomes unwittingly associated with a theoretical limit, for we are unable to understand the natural dissolution that is presumed to appear at the breakdown of civil law.

True, that outcome least desirable to our foreclosed civil schedule of expectations irresistibly appears most shocking. But if the intensity of shock, allowing for summary formulation, is expressed in inverse ratio to the routinized force of antecedent expectations of tranquillity, it is necessary to distinguish the civil *incentive* from the *rational justification* of those expectations.

If we fail to do this, we shall continue to seal the problem out from the negotiable range of sustained thought, continue to treat the physical violence done to our established conventions as tantamount to a convulsive "violence" inflicted upon the abstract prospect of intelligent scrutiny. We would be forced by our premises to conclude that assertions about violent derangement are themselves violently deranged, as if a chemist assumed that his propositions on the content of alcohol were themselves alcoholic. That this *reductio* has never been carried through from the premises of the traditional account only reveals that the resolution of our prepossessions regarding the question of violence has been uncritically overruled by our containing bias for civil order, notwithstanding the conceptual order entailed by it.

It is traditional to view civil society as conserving and violence as dissipating. Those who uphold the established coordinates of the institutional structure are called conservatives, and those who bring it down, radicals. Extreme Left and Right are described as dissipates. Politics characterizes the axis of oscillation between conservation and dissipation. This view — however necessary as a form of consolation in a world whose very modernity and sophistication is haunted by continuing fear of climactic disintegration — misrepresents the fundamental tenets of political order.

What is perhaps noteworthy here is that violent behavior is ascribed to solitary disposition conceived either in microcosm as an isolated, unruly chaos of individual combats, everybody against everybody, or in the international arena as anthropomorphic isolation of the gladiatorial Leviathan. The *social* character of violent relation is, quite remarkably, absent in both dimensions of Hobbes' classic analysis. How is the lapse to be explained?

I believe that it may ultimately be derived from the illicit mental construction that is called the anthropomorphic or organismic fallacy, by which we ascribe the physiological and anatomical properties of human individuals to some indefinite aggregate, the operations of which, lacking this metaphor, are not otherwise easily discernible to human understanding.

In his introduction to *Leviathan*, Hobbes sets out his political order as an "Artificiall Man,"

> though of greater stature than the naturall, for whose protection and defence it was intended; and in which, the *Soveraignty* is an Artificiall Soul, as giving life and motion to the whole body; the Magistrates ... artificiall *Joynts*; *Reward and Punishment* ... are the *Nerves*, that do the same in the Body Naturall.

This "artificial" construction exaggerates, on the one hand, the integral relations of the domestic membership of the polity, and on the other, the independence of the "body" politic vis-à-vis its counterparts in the universal state of nature.

What is significant for my argument is that the sovereign appears in the external environment as a lone duellist, poised for action, ready to deal and receive the cudgels and bruises in battle, risking by this personification "his" violent death. The efficacy of this purely illusionary construction on our imaginations should not be underestimated.

The image effectively masks the risk of the contained members of society who, notwithstanding their "embodiment" in the personified sovereign and the protection of his gargantuan shield, must by any rational account enter the field and bear the brunt of war. It is the citizenry, after all, not the fictive sovereign body, that receives the fatal wound. Thus our gaze is distracted from the gravity of the risk assumed by the membership so long as we gaze at the metaphoric screen on which the solitary Leviathan is projected, eyes fixed, weapon pointed in the "posture of war." The obvious flaw is that while the posture may be abstractly embodied in the persona of the ruler, in practice it is the individual citizen, and not the sovereign, who is struck by the bullet.

Hobbes' illusion is further consonant with the utter formlessness of the international environment in his system, despite the critical relation of that environment to the welfare of the members. Hobbes assumes the structure of the duel, an outstanding difference between two (duo) individuals or collectives that can be settled only by recourse to arms. (Actually, the Latin word *bellum* derives from the antique *duellem*.) Not only is the interaction with the rival commonwealth unrepresented but the nature of that interaction is suspended, despite the critical relation of that engagement to the *domestic* welfare of the membership.

The process and consequences of violent engagement cannot be closely examined because the equal and opposing counterpart sovereign appears in the remotest margin of the Leviathan's political universe. There is duel but no second commonwealth. This absence is presumed in the very form of political discourse, both classical and modern. *The Republic, The Leviathan, The Social Contract*: the proper name and its functional equivalent, the definite article "the," as in the political system, manifestly reveal singular foci of political cognizance. Political order has a dual commitment in referring to the environment of at least two nations, otherwise it would be impossible to make sense of those losses suffered by the domestic membership of either state.

If for the purposes of external welfare, however, the Leviathan appears as a singular structure, a pseudo body, the violent challenge emanating from within the civil order is viewed as pathologic, that is, structureless. If the organic fallacy exaggerates the independence of the body politic abroad, it conversely denies all structure to the violent challenge emerging from within its capacious body, glimpsed then as a contra-natural dissolution into a confused multitude. The one great pseudo body breaks down into the unnatural, intestinal disorder of an unruly individual body, into irregular convulsions of corporeal atoms, opaque and windowless, but unlike the monads in Leibniz's universe, they explode into a state of preestablished disharmony. Hobbes leaps from one great body to a set of stunted bodies.

Thus if the artificial person imagined by Hobbes conceals the role of the membership in foreign war, it further denies all structure to insurgent forces in civil war by formulating its outbreak as contra-natural dissolution. Once admitting the functional status of the contrived pseudo body, it follows that all internal attacks may be viewed, however phantasmagorically, as atomizing diseases. I will designate this contrivance as the pathologic fallacy. Clearly, if we reflect on the question dispassionately, a revolutionary community cannot be considered, *prima facie*, as a variety of "convulsive excrescence." It would place quite a strain on credibility.

The organic fallacy operates in two complementary directions: it hallows obligation on the analogy to corporeal integrity in foreign war, and stigmatizes civil insurrection on the analogy to coporeal disability. Nor should we view this construction as a merely picturesque manner of speaking. The assumption that the outbreak of violence is coterminous with a contagious infection remains, down to our own day, a chronic conviction of Western thought.

The "disease" has proved to be more subtle in the present ("The Anatomy of Revolution," "The Etiology of Internal War, "The *Pathology* of the Legal System"), but political scientists and historians find it difficult to move themselves from the seat of medical judgment, however futile their diagnoses have been in providing some viable relief from violent illness plaguing the feverish body politic. When a philosophic orientation remains inveterate, one cannot afford to view its manifestation as merely metaphoric or light-hearted in intent, especially when it mystifies our understanding of a subject of critical import. To assume that neither writers who treat violence as pseudo-organic illness nor their audience, take this approach seriously, is to wed oneself to a very common, but for all that, very misleading confidence. There is no greater illusion in treatments of social subjects than the conviction that we have exorcised our illusions.

Indeed, it may be argued that it is the characteristic predicament of all attempts to shed some welcome light on this question that their authors have denied a coherent structure to their subject at the precise moment they have attempted an orderly investigation of it. Their constructions generally not only defined the agencies of violence out of rational control, but in the process also built in the structural failure of their theoretical composition so far as it can only yield "a void in society" in the observer's extrapolated picture. The problem is not only the assertion of blindness in the designated agents, but an assertion in blindness by the designating observer composing one blank transparency over another ad infinitum.

Thus it has been well nigh impossible to make even a start toward thorough-going inquiry under the aegis of the traditional formulations, no more than a watercolorist can even begin to paint a marinescape on the surface of the sea. The difficulty when confronting the problem of violence seems then not too dissimilar to Augustine's perplexity in formulating the concept of time: "I lose thee when I seek to find thee out." The difference between we moderns and the Bishop of Hippo is that we have not faced the anomalous consequences of our patent assumptions regarding the critical question. We have not undertaken a candid but unavoidably vexing reexamination of first principles.

It is not surprising then that despite the recognition on all sides that the problem of violence in modern society represents the gravest threat to elevated human purpose, despite the grievous concern the problem has always raised at all levels of culture, academic or otherwise, it has never — not in the course of Western intellectual development — received general or systematic treatment, free of both the question-begging compunctions of civil intelligence and the equally mistaken reaction engendered by them. Here I mean the impetuous "irrationalist" propensities of the heroic imagination, given voice by the epic philosophers of the fin-de-siècle: Nietzsche, Sorel, Bergson, and in somewhat truncated form, by Freud.

This ensemble invoked, by reverse but equally resourceless complement to the civicentric view, the apocalyptic breakout from the containing and constricting norms of civil society viewed in such counter-provocative terms as the deracinating état postiche. Consequently, their novel perspective was foregrounded, not as a mythic *abomination* of chaos, but as a liberating *apotheosis* of chaos. Thus Nietzsche puts forward his uncontained and "unfathomable" will-to-power and Bergson his mystique of the explosive and boundless *élan vital*, free of all secular confinement, erupting like a "*coup d'état* of the mind" or like "a [cannon] shell that suddenly bursts into fragments" which in turn burst again into smaller pieces. As life proceeds along these lines, the author of *Creative Evolution* instructs us "to take things by storm, you must thrust intelligence outside itself by an act of will."

Sorel, in turn, explicitly adapting Bergson's biological indeterminism to the arena of social forces, proclaims the "unanalyzable" myth of the general strike projected only in the abandonment of combat as "epic-consciousness," a claim that renders his very "reflections" on the problem of violence altogether problematic to critical scrutiny, if not paradoxical in its own terms.

Finally, we encounter Freud's sobering version, which while hardly celebrating the heroic will to violence, nonetheless invests it with the "self-subsistent," i. e., the irreducible significance of the "death-instinct." Far from remaining ministerial to civilizing constraint, it assumes an "autonomous" status in Freud's meta-psychology, and far from appearing as a pathologic aberration may, by service to the goal of climactically "reinstating [the] antecedent inorganic state," be considered as a therapeutic objective of the organism. This invocation of a death instinct yields a harvest of paradox by assuming an inscrutable teleological mode of instinctual satisfaction that terminates the otherwise life conserving, or in negative terms, death averting functions, of the instincts. Then how is it possible to impose conceptual limits to an instinct that eliminates instincts?

Summing up, however incompatible the civil and epic orientations, both are given over to the presupposition that once the dynamic of violence breaks out and away from the ministrations of civil control, be that control formulated in moral, psychological, or strategic terms, its course, whether abominated or celebrated, is presumed at the same moment to fall outside the scope and surveyable limits of human reason.

How then can we speak sensibly to a topic that can be reformulated by paraphrase as the structure of destruction ?

Indeed, could any formulation stand in clearer incompatibility with the fundamental assumption of modern political thought, made explicit by Hobbes, that the cohesive force of human society is invariably generated as a repulsion to violence and its most appealing consequence — premature death?

We are therefore well taught that the conservation of civil order is negatively related to unrestrained belligerence and constituted precisely as a refuge from the gross fear of violent death. The aversive reaction to that terrible prospect is conceived as sufficient to deliver the binding energy of the social bond qua social bond.

It follows conversely, that if the disposition to fatal risk so far from repelling, attracts the membership across the threshold of violent exchange, a "contra-natural dissolution" of social bond ensues, bringing down the house, engendering the catastrophic "war of everybody against everybody," leaving in its wake, in the memorable words of Hobbes, "no place for industry ... no culture on the earth ... no commodious buildings ... no knowledge on the face of the earth; no account of time; no arts; no letters; no society; and which is worst of all, continual fear and danger of violent death; and the life of man solitary, poor, nasty, brutish and short."

The considered form of this counteracting union has characteristically disclosed a dominant metaphor, however varied its theoretical design, ancient or modern, through the long course of political and social thought; I mean the convention of the container, conceived as insulating its putative membership within (by reference to its domestic jurisdiction) from the arbitrary dangers of violent death and isolating that unmediated danger without to the *terra incognita* of exogenous and chaotic battle.

After the fall of the Roman Republic in the 1st century B. C., the severe distinction between violence and war was treated with a certain lassitude. Today we employ these terms interchangeably. We will therefore want to know why this distinction, once viewed as critical, was subsequently lost to the scrutiny of Western political thought.

What use then did the Romans make of violentia and bellum? Violence derives from *vis*, connoting vehemence or inordinate energy. But the two cognates branching off from this root complicate the meaning. *Violentus* describes the intensity of an action, as in Cicero: "I know this man's frenzy, I know his unbridled violence" (*Novi hominis furorum, novi effranatum violentiam*). Here vehement behavior is not yet illicit conduct. Clearly one may shout vehemently without breaking the law; nonetheless *vis* also yields *violatio*, the manifest violation of a sacred prohibition or legal rule. Thus Cicero declares: "There shall be a penalty for the violation of law" (*poena violati juris esto*).

To be sure, violent behavior by intensification and exaggeration of normal conduct may produce violation. It requires an unusual exertion of energy to inflict a grave and unlawful injury; but, on the other hand, all vehement exertion is not unlawful injury. Even at the extreme, the laying of a "lesion grave" on another is not *a priori* illicit. Indeed, taking the life of an enemy *in bello* outside the *locus Romanus* was not only considered legitimate but altogether honorific. The victim must be identified as a citizen before *violatio* can be ascribed to the act. If the intensity and gravity of violence supplies only the necessary condition, then the context of the slaying and the identity of the slain provide the sufficient ground for *violatio*.

Our very concept of politics described by the surrounding ring-wall of the Greek polis, bounding the membership as if within a tightened vessel, expelling violence beyond the legal and topographic enclosure, assumes the indentured container as the cardinal convention of all derived knowledge on political matters. But our bias for containing civil order is most clearly seen in the law and rhetoric of the Roman republic and the sacred denominations of *domi et militiae*.

The domestic sanctuary constituted the locus of peaceful negotiation characterized at best by gracious magnanimity, but at least, as prudent reserve. On the other side, the field of honor stipulated the locus of pious battle characterized at best by spirited audacity, but at least, as steadfastness within the ranks. It will be recognized that these terms imply both a mutually exclusive set of locations, the site of refuge and the site of battle, and a set of dispositions appropriate to them, the animus civilis and the *animus bellicus*. Under the constitution of the Roman republic, the domicile described the area of protected citizenship, whose interlocking privileges presupposed that its members were sacrosanct, constitutionally inviolable, and enjoyed the status of forbidden targets. The *militiae* comprehended the precinct outside the containing walls of the sanctuary, the zone of licensed human-slaying undertaken against the alien suffering the status of prescribed target. On these terms, it is evident that the disposition expected in battle is incompatible with the demeanor appropriate to the civil refuge. If homicide is understood as honorific on campaign, its commission, on the other hand, within the domicile is translated as utter abomination, calling for the severest penalty.

Accordingly, home and battlefield are not obviously congruent with the conventional division of home and work; for despite the Victorian ideal of the "domestic refuge" from the competitive playing field of male-dominated work activities, the obligations assumed alternately in the familial residence and at the site of professional service were always clearly recognized as compatible aliases within the civil locus. By contrast, the ecological divisions of *domi et militiae* and the respective dispositions attached to them, stand in a relation of mutual exclusion. If political society coordinately includes the civil and military sectors under the requirements of custodial maintenance and defense, it should be noted that by exclusive contrast with all other specialized functionaries in the domestic division of labor, the disposition of the armed service is uniquely destructive and therefore necessarily assumes its responsibility outside the sanctuary.

For example, if physicians, pursuant to their Hippocratic oath, can serve their sponsor and patient in the single person of their fellow citizen, the warriors must by the stern mandate of their martial oath divorce the person of their civil sponsor on behalf of whom they are commissioned from the person of their alien patient upon whom they apply their martial skills. To save the former they are obliged to kill the latter, not as a misadventure of surgical incision, not as a merciful response to unsalvageable injury, but as a direct imperative of their military posture. Here the warrior is at once included as a servile instrument, but excluded by explicit performance of his characteristic function.

Thus by way of the two-fold exorcism of violence, alienated on the one hand at a benign legal distance as deviant, and hence extraordinary acts of violation, or exported on the other hand as removed acts of war at an edifying territorial distance, the polity endures as an exclusive sanctuary. It hedges in the disposition of the civil membership, the conduct of which is strictly regulated by reference to the corporate objective of peace and safety; a polity flourishing, as it were, in a sealed container, under a privileged immunity, free from the gross, if not the marginal disturbances, of wayward violence. As Cicero declared, the citizens are insulated from within by the "awe of the law and law courts," and isolated from without by the circumscribing boundary. Mommsen's remark, that Roman citizens viewed their station within the privileged Eternal City as if they were securely situated within a "closed chamber," makes precisely this point.

Nonetheless, it is allowed even in their purely abstract conventions or historical settings that these corporations are susceptible to precipitate atomization and radical decomposition in the face of two equally but sudden accidents of civil order — however ideally conceived that order may be by constitution — and that is in the event of internal revolution or external invasion. These crises may be more manageably articulated if we recognize that the containing structures dividing the political range between domi and militiae are given over to collapse under either one or both of these grievous conditions. Both domestic rebellion and foreign invasion represent the breakdown of the delimiting boundary between the sanctuary and the battlefield, and, at the same time, represent the collapse of the antithetical legal denominations, criminal homicide and just war, contingent upon the maintenance of the split ecological jurisdictions.

Clearly, at these decisive junctures the process of violence can no longer be relegated outside the law by the threat of judicial punishment, nor exported beyond the walls by magisterial discipline. Whether conceived as originating from the direction of the domicile as insurrection, or viewed as originating from the militiae as invasion, these vicissitudes reduce the boundary separating the privileged refuge of civil negotiation and the ruinous field of alien battle to an unpartitioned and uncontained frontier of conflict. As Lucan morosely resigns the Roman civil wars: "Inseparably crowding together the assembly of man and the lairs of beasts." At what point, then, do the cross-cutting calamities of civil war and/or foreign invasion indiscriminately confound the abominable homicide of the endogenous refuge with the honorable human-slaying of the external field of honor?

It is not clear that under these harrowing conditions "the noble and the base are butchered together," as Augustine invokes the decimating spectacle of Sulla's revolutionary proscription, "not in formal justice nor by order of law but all in confusion." At that moment, the warrior, so far from exercising his craft on behalf of his fellow citizens against the prescribed alien, administers his skills upon his otherwise inviolable constituents. Do not the criminal and the warrior assume, at that juncture, a common identity as the citizen and the alien are put on a corresponding

90 Violence and Utopia

level of unprivileged equality, the equality of sufferance? Here is, as recorded by Lucan, the image of Caesar exhorting his troops to the act of mass fratricide, to indiscriminate violence: "And whoever finds himself driving his sword through a kinsman's heart ... must take credit for this act, which in any other circumstance would be a crime; the credit will be the same whether your opponent is a stranger or not, because no difference can be made between one enemy and another."

Rather than appearing as external perturbation or manageable deviation outside the legal boundary, the process of violence assumes at the outbreak of insurrection a normative status within the domicile proper. Correspondingly, at the shocking breakthrough of invasion, the battle, instead of remaining a remote exigency of the militiae, appears as the intransigently proximate disposition at the very seat of sanctuary. In a word, indifferent to civil constraint, insurrection generalizes crime beyond the underworld, as invasion generalizes war beyond the battlefield.

But once admitting that the violent disposition cannot be contained by location (despite inevitable attempts to maintain a facade of "business-as-usual"), nor harnessed as functional "means" to civil purpose in the massive breach of the authorizing residence, then the civil terms parcelling out violence in small as deviant criminality and removed acts of war are deprived of any sensible correspondence. They cannot, by definition, provide objective explanation of the gravest events that belie them, revolution and invasion.

Hence the requirements of a general inquiry into violence are always greater than the level of analysis permitted by the container convention, always greater and indeed systematically excluded by the contracted bounds of the fractional association. Under these circumstances, it is hardly surprising that precisely when the question of violence is evoked, not in its deviant and circumstantial form, but in its normative and unextenuated prominence, that we are advised by the traditional instruction that nothing is evident but a chaotic decomposition of social structure into "a war of everybody against everybody" for the duration of the breach. And that is to say no more than that the question is abandoned precisely when it is most serious.

Here we face the unbending but brittle disjunction of our theoretical design: the rigidity of a crystalline order, expelling violence beyond its enclosed boundaries, or a precipitate collapse and boundless disorder; a hyperstructured container or a structureless chaos. On the one hand, we are offered a unique solution that divides away the question, on the closed spatial dissociation of the civicentric orientation, to the putative distance of the "underworld" or the remote precincts of the battlefield. As a consequence of that move, violence is relieved of the appearance of a critical problem; its manifestations are immediately gainsaid by relegation to its specially conceived limbos. The problem on this axis is precluded from appearing as a problem, since its custodial solution, after all, goes in advance of it, leaving the core society of decent citizens securely invested in their commodious routines, veritably untouched by its "isolated" upshot attained by an alternate, illicit route. On these terms, the problem may be construed as a "latent function" hitched to the upward spiral of net social productivity. The water the cow drinks, however contaminated, inexorably turns to milk.

On the other hand, if the violent incidents multiply beyond some conventionally assumed but hardly specifiable limit, its outbreak is then projected in terms of an all-consuming apocalypse discontinuous with and detached from the temporal boundaries of the civil schedule of expectations. And this conceived rupture then appears too confounding for any but the most insupportably deranging outcome, total dissolution in the Hobbesian sense. But on either condition it will be recognized that the question is begged: on the first by its relegated insignificance; on the second by resignation to unintelligible distention.

An act of violence, however injurious, does not qualify as an act of violation unless the putative capacity for rational choice or intention can be ascribed to its agency. Violation here will be defined provisionally as an intentional act by one agent to injure another in his or her person or possessions against the other's will. Presumably it is the normative objective of the law to minimize if not altogether prevent the incidents of these actions by attaching punitive sequels to their execution. The gravity of the outcome determines the severity of the punishment, assuming that both the crime and the punitive value attached to it are not only previously recorded in the tablet of the laws but transcribed and well established in common usage.

The charged significance of location on the Roman distinction between violence and violation is seen in the ancient division of *domi et militiae*, home and field. Humanslaying in the one constitutes an *illicit* act of violence, but the identical behavior in the other is accepted as the *licit* act of war. Hence the division between home and field serves to designate an action as either *violatio* or *bellum*. The distinction still obtains in the modern era, creating a fundamental contradiction in the ethical behavior of collective human society. If A can kill alien B but not co-citizen C, we may call the violent relation intransitive. If A must kill foreigner B but must not kill co-citizen C, A stands in an intransitive relation to B and C because he cannot carry over his disposition from the one to the other. He can neither be non-violent to B nor violent to C without suffering severe penalty for the breach of either rule. If A refuses to do battle with B on the ground that we do not have a special but general relation to humankind and that one life cannot be privileged over another, A exposes him or herself to reprisal by the same state that would also punish him or her for doing to C what he or she would hesitate to do to B. In this sense, both the pacifist and the felon share outlaw status. These diametrically opposed references to violent conduct presuppose that the political order, by constitution, is based on a split culture.

This arises from the problematics of the origins of civil societies: the state of nature is not left behind when humans "enter" civil society; it is, more precisely, transposed to the foreign environment. Thus the members are at once "in" and "out" of the state of nature, or put the other way around, "in" and "out" of civil society. If a state of war prevails in this environment, the membership may as a matter of constitutional obligation be called upon to risk their lives for a society whose very rationale for sovereign existence is to get the members, to use the words of Hobbes, "out of that miserable condition of war" and the condition invested with the "terror of present death." In the end, it is the safety of life and limb "where of all sovereignty was ordained" in the first instance.

The civil authority, the guarantor of life, may send the citizens to their death on a foreign field. Although the victims fall on terra incognita, beyond the bounds of civil domicile, this does not, for all that, alter their identity: they are the self-same citizens who "when they assembled to make a common representative ... one by one ...promised obedience" that they might receive in turn "their lives." The sovereign then empowered to save his subjects from the state of nature may turn about and return them to the state of nature, i. e., the "terror of present death," subverting in that moment the justification of civil society for the recruited combatants in the first place.

The Leviathan wielding the sword lets loose the state of nature, so to speak, within itself.

The members who cross the threshold to enter civil society do not, as one is inclined to suppose, open a conventional swinging door to get "out" of a state of nature, closing it behind them, setting down then in a commodious chamber. The citizen has, in fact, to put the prevailing metaphor right, inserted himself in a revolving door which takes him out of the state of nature into civil society, and out again to a state of nature, without ever releasing the membership from the cyclical dynamic imposed by the dual obligations — civil and military.

The standing military obligation, inextricably wedded to civil society qua civil society, presupposes that there is no structural breakdown of society attendant upon the demanded risk of violent death, whatever its justification. However we wish to conceal the awful consequences of that apparently "external" or remote environment within the "internal" safety net of the domestic constituents, it is nevertheless undeniable that the ostensibly exotic state of nature is not introduced as an extraordinary disruption of the course of events, but as a "continual" and normative, that is, structured liability of individuals, wherever situated, and however apparently detached from that danger to the untenable but embracing walls of the corporate container.

The civil order, not by structural default, but by constitution, requires, in structured alteration, the prudent aversion and the impetuous risk of violent death.

The container convention assumes that violent behavior and its consequences reverse the pursued direction of the homo civilis, designed to obtain refuge from violent death and injury. In fact, political obligation does not put us "inside" or "outside" of any preconceived establishment metaphorically considered as housing civil society. A priori, no set of individuals are either "in" or "out" of civil society, for they are not at all parts of a univocal structure. It is not a matter of disjunctive choice, made in advance, between a society constituted of "members" organically bound by exaggerated integration to civil society, or the pathological dismemberment and exaggerated dissociation of a state of nature tantamount to a *null society*. It is not a question of either a container or a chaos. We are not individuals or members of the greater individual "writ large," nor dis-members of it. Nor or we "in" or "out" of the Leviathan "body politic," nor "in" any social system or pathologically out of it.

On the one hand, we conceptualize the civil institutions of associations based on the interdependent operations of the division of labor as enjoining — following the model of the containing organic connection and flexion of the musculature — the restricted antagonism and hence, limited liability, of the members within the body politic. These limiting conditions are perceived as the very conditions that structure the protracted negotiation and possible renegotiation of conflicts in a context of augmented productivity and permanent association. This construction presupposes the confinement of social activity to at most attenuated contests, exemplified by the bargain in the commercial process and the dialogue in the rhetorical process, contests waged by restriction as "price wars" and as "logomachy," or "war of words," when these exchanges may not be described benignly as exemplary acts of magnanimous charity or as gentle deliberations of disinterested inquiry.

On the other hand, if in contrast to the reconcilable antagonism and extended dealings of civil life we set out the process of violence between unrestrained belligerents in terms of a) unlimited bestiality (with reference to the means, entailing a brief fight to the finish with fatal rather than civil "weapons") and b) uncontained and indiscriminate brawl with respect to targets ("a war of everybody against everybody"), we are presented with types of confrontations that far from perpetuating, irreversibly terminate, the possibility of a negotiable meeting. Indeed, they represent a "meeting" designed to end all meetings. The exacted cost of interaction between the armed belligerents — with the exception of uneasy truces — is the sudden elimination of one or both parties to it, disposed as they are to "kill or die" at the moment they attain the zone of contact. "There where someone stood only a moment ago stands no one at all."

The expression "outbreak" so often attached to violence seems remarkably appropriate, for the violent act represents an extraordinary breakout from a closed series of self-sufficient and complementary civil gestures in seemingly perpetual motion. It renders all the manifold expressions of civil negotiation inoperative for the duration of contact.

It should not seem surprising that when we accent our grasp of violent acts by reference to the rhetorical exclamations evoked at their inception, e.gs., "unbelievable," "incredible," "horrible," we are implying that civil intelligence, all the more as it is refined, has unwittingly equated the violation of domestic law and etiquette with the suspension of the orderly processes of nature. It is as if the breakdown of civil law was seen to be no less incredible, no less unintelligible than the sudden and unexplained suspension of the laws of conservation of matter and energy operating in the physical world. Thus Hobbes and Burke perceived the eruption of violence as a chaos, an apocalyptic void in the social organism.

By contrast with the consequences of violent deed, the fundamental forms of secular action are reversible: the unemployed worker may be rehired, the divorced man or woman may remarry, the religious apostate may convert or return to the fold of the faithful. But the preeminent effect of violence, sudden death, is *irreversible*. For the deceased the act can neither be repeated nor undone, and as such constitutes the absolute limit of human action.

The violent process, moreover, does not distinguish the production of nature from the artifacts of human manufacture. Both the century-old forest and the mansion that required a year to construct are indifferently consumed in the flame and their previous history cannot be read in the ashes. The agency of violence so far as it does not respect the previous time path of its targets breaks down the otherwise distinctive separation of the manifest species of physis from the manifest construction of *techne,* critical to the Aristotelian formulation.

Accordingly, a violent process abbreviates the duration of a given contact when the engaged elements might have otherwise persisted for an indefinite period of association. On the other hand, if the process of violence did not prima facie discriminate the history of its objects in terms of nature or artifice, its destruction could be equally effected by the agency of human action, the use of a weapon, or the blind ferocity of nature, as in the cases of earthquake and volcanic eruption.

Thus it is important to emphasize at the outset that violence conceptualizes both the advertent effort of human intervention by way of a weapon or the inadvertent so-called "acts of nature." If the objects of violence cannot be confined to the products of human creation, neither can they be restricted at its source merely to the malice of human agency. The extensive processes of natural growth, human fabrication, as well as human life may be brought down one and all during the brief but intense duration of violence. In this sense, violence includes all those agencies that interrupt the protracted and graduated time line of natural maturation or fabricated durability, and relatively slow decay or wear and tear attending their development or use. It may be argued then that violence is premature death or decomposition of an identifiable object; for, excluding the intervention of that radical vicissitude the object would have otherwise endured for an indefinite subsequent period of time. This foreshortening by violence of the natural processes of growth and durability or premature violent death may be understood as a death *killing* death! — that is, the sudden acceleration of the normally slow degradation of biological senescence.

If violence radically accelerates the process of decomposition it could only be perceived because there is an identifiable object that it attacks. Far from indicating homogeneity and chaos, that is, a condition under which construction and destruction are interchangeable, all violence presupposes at the point of human observation a sudden threat in the form of abrupt changes in motion to objects ordinarily undergoing slow orderly transition. An act of violence always requires a relatively stable target that moves sufficiently orderly to be recognized by human perception prior to the attack upon it. On the other hand, if both the products of phased processes of growth and the gauged operation of human technique are vulnerable to violence and equally qualifiable as targets, neither can the source of violence in either nature or human conduct be discriminated.

The concept of violence inevitably comprehends more than the category of weapons. Correspondingly, the "means of violence," or more properly, the means of violent expression, presupposes some quiddity beyond the reference to the potential inherent in the state's warehouse of armaments. A sword or a crossbow cannot be meaningfully equated with a weapons-system, legitimate or illegitimate, as Weber incorrectly assumed. Indeed, Weber compounded this error because he not only mistakenly equated the means of violence with a weapons- system, but even more narrowly identified the means of violence with a specialized apparatus "monopolized" and inventoried by the ordnance function of the government stockpile. (Weber is not alone in his confusion, but shares this misconception with many professional scholars of political science, sociology, and military strategy.)

Contrary to the widely mistaken assumption, any and all manipulatable objects in the human environment, either in a natural or constructed state, can become "weapons" or "means of violence" narrowly conceived. The limb of a tree, a stone, a club, a chair, the pencil I write with and the paper I write upon, and even (giving vent to the disturbing recollection of Richard III) the pillow upon which I sit, can all be used as weapons — however less efficient they may be than a rifle or a bomb — depending upon the disposition of their agent at any given moment. If my readers will only cast their eyes about the immediate environment, they will not discover a solitary object that cannot be employed, despite enormous variation in scale and texture, as a means of destruction.

The generic concept of violence is decidedly more comprehensive in its range than the category of weapons, refined or crude, with which it is traditionally associated. When our attention is directed to the performance of a violent act we are disposed to assume that a discrete and clearly delineated activity has been undertaken requiring a special inclination or aptitude comparable to well denominated exercises like speaking, walking, jogging, swimming, eating, etc. But on closer scrutiny do we not recognize on the contrary that these latter efforts may be performed violently? Clearly one may speak violently (with oratorical bombast); walk violently (consider a high-stepping march); swim violently (in the proximity of sharks); and eat violently (when wolfing down comestibles). Violence and moderation are not predicated correctly on an exemplary need, but are terms modifying the expression of all activities undertaken with any intense effort.

Our capacity for violence is presupposed by our capacity to move, and it follows that there are as many ways of acting notwithstanding the purposive, reflexive, or purely inadvertent articulation of that action. We are therefore prepared to accept as axiomatic that there is nothing that can be done that cannot conceivably be done violently. Conversely, there is nothing that can be done that cannot conceivably be performed with moderation. It does not seem possible to confine the concept of violence, however less problematic it appears in that secure formulation, as one more special proclivity in the classified repertoire of human aptitudes, nor may it be understood as a self-sufficient "destructive" or "aggressive" instinct in Freud's terms, contrasted by way of competition with the hunger or sexual drives. In fact, as we have seen with other basic human activities, hunger pangs and sexual tension may on their own terms be satisfied violently. Violent behavior cannot be detached or separated from any possible inclination for it is a conditional phase of all physical acts. Violent behavior then is not like one additional piano key tacked on to the end of a row of discrete predecessors — the last key faced down, the ultimo ratio finally discharged, if you will, upon the instrument; for indeed, each and every key on the board may be impressed *piano* or *forte*, softly or vehemently, gently or violently.

But if the range of violent expression cannot be restricted to a certain privileged temper, aptitude, or art, it will follow that its execution does not depend upon and therefore cannot be equated with any specialized "means." Our problem, in other words, may not be understood as Weber would have it, by narrow reference to a peculiar "means of violence" or weapons system. Violence is not a resource but a mode of expression and thus all products of nature may be used violently.

Plutarch's parable, "The boys kill the frogs for sport, but the frogs die in earnest," illuminates another crucial aspect of violence. The innocence of the illustration is not designed to belie the gravity of the problem: the significance of violence is *decisively determined by the identity of the observer and the perspective from whence he or she views the target.* The signification of violence cannot be given *a priori* by the identity of the species homo sapiens but depends upon the political identity of the victim. The disparity of attitude reflected in the contrasting standpoints of victor and victim mirrors the inconsistency of the social demands connected with the sacred segregation of *domi* and *militiae*. When, for example, the bombing of Guernica is viewed from the distraught focus of Picasso's sensibility, it reveals the unmollified expression of the monstrous in human guise. But when viewed from the cockpit of the attacking aircraft by one of Mussolini's pilots, it discloses a heightened "aesthetic" experience describing the movement of fleeing refugees as delicate patterns midst "wonderful arabesques of smoke." Where Picasso contrives by aesthetic means to communicate the moral abomination of violence, the pilot produces the violence to create an aesthetic effect!

In sum, any object in the environment can become an instrument of violence. There is no specialized monopoly of the means, although the potential capacity for inflicting damage varies considerably among individuals and nations. Everyone is physically capable of violence, symbolized in the notion of the levée en masse in which every ablebodied male citizen is expected to participate in battle not as a matter of choice but of obligation. Everyone is capable of committing homicide, where ability does not necessarily imply skill as in the case of the professional hit man. It follows that violence is not just a special resource or exotic capacity, but a generic alternative of human action realizable in any given individual in any possible social system, large or small, primitive or advanced. Paradoxically, the modern nation-state has learned how to institutionalize and exploit certain forms of violence as instruments of control.

Civilization exacts from its inhabitants more than they can possibly provide. Always striving to push the limitations of nature further back beyond the walls of the polis, the civil order exacts a vast and uninterrupted flow of energy from its constituents and channels it into activities that do not threaten its internal stability. The surpassing norms encourage individuals to rise in the hierarchy of accomplishment, and the restraining norms compel them to abide by the limitations that insure its fundamental obligation to the membership of reduced bodily risk. Structural ambiguities obtain from the contradictions in competitive civil society in which the demand for success inevitably leads to violations of the norms: to advance the ideals of the civil order it becomes necessary to resort in secret (or openly in structurally privileged areas) to the most flagrant transgressions upon the social codes of decorum and morality.

Growing out of the social contradictions of civil society is the fraternal order with its ethos of violence — fraternity constituting an alternative affiliative mode. Although the civil order may create fraternal adjuncts such as the police to maintain domestic stability and expeditionary forces to suppress other societies in the name of self-defense, the fraternal order exists in dialectical opposition to the civil order. Indeed, the two structures operate simultaneously in a state of mutual tension and mutual interdependence.

Contrary to the circumstances of safety and non-injurious interaction aimed for within the civil order, the fraternal association courts extreme danger not as a last resort, but as a positive value to be wrested from existence, indeed, to be provoked if absent. Thus Thucydides has Pericles exhort: "Remember that where dangers are greatest there the greatest honors are to be won." The violent engagement, however, upon which honor flourishes, precipitates the most unpredictable consequences in the environment. The longer the process of violence continues, the less reliable appear those judgments formed at the outbreak of the struggle.

Yet it is precisely the radical environmental instability that provides the "proof" and "verification" of comradely fidelity. The fraternal demonstration of affiliation based on confrontation with another inverts, quite strikingly, the meaning of "evidence" so far as that term is construed in scientific discourse. The latter depends upon the constraint of uncertainty in order to "test" or "verify" under controlled conditions contingent predictions presuming an infinitely extensible future of subsequent tests supplying instances of reconfirmation or disconfirmation of the provisional hypothesis.

The fraternal community requires, on the contrary, the uncontrolled environmental condition, the radical unknown, par excellence: violent, that is, premature death. If the depth of a person's intelligence is tested by his or her knowledge of a defined environment, in the case of the warrior a person's depth of affiliation is tested by the willingness to face that contingency that escapes all human knowledge, the immanent possibility of violent death, on behalf of the defined comrade(s), and this test may be applied whenever and wherever that fatal danger is made manifest, be it direct confrontation with an enemy on the terra incognita of the foreign battlefield or the domestic barricades, whether that be sought by *active* aggression or by *passive reception* (the non-violent martyr threatens his or her enemy by unilaterally risking the destruction of his own body).

The fraternal order structures itself to eliminate ambiguity in social relations. It owes its existence to the willingness of its members to confront situations where death yields a zero degree of potential surprise and thus sacrifice themselves for the sake of the rest. This unites them in common struggle and forges bonds between them that know no equal in civil society. The fraternity demands unequivocal loyalty of its members and enforces strict standards of obligation toward fraternal goals. Rather than attempt to avoid the risk of violent death as in the civil order, the membership courts it in the fraternal mode as a way of certifying honesty and commitment to the group ethos. Hence the membership is always secure in their being regarding their status among the membership. Whereas in civil society agreements must be legally acknowledged in the form of contracts witnessed by third parties, in the fraternal structure commitment is expressed directly through the medium of the oath. The duplicity and dissimulation inevitably leading to the weak social relations of the civil order are replaced with the ultimate proof of affiliation in the form of confrontation with death. If the prime expression of social and commercial exchange in civil society is the bargain, in the fraternal structure it takes the form of the duel.

The duel serves the coactive function of conserving the intensive relationship by risk as opposed to the bargain, which sacrifices the intensive relationship in order to augment capital accumulation, the extensive purpose of the interaction.

The male-dominated fraternal order offers the possibility of proof of commitment as well as of masculinity. Paradoxically, in modern technological societies masculinity is not proven through manual strength but by possession of a weapon. It may be claimed that the weapon substitutes for masculinity in an indolent culture. Yet the question is less about what one fights against than about for whom one fights. The condition of friendship within the fraternal order is not necessarily hostility against another human agency, for there are alternative life-risking means of demonstrating affiliation. The pitting of one's life against the indifferent forces of nature — mountain climbing, perilous adventures on land and sea and in air and space — comprise a series of challenges that test one's metal in the circle of close companions. Why do human beings prefer to do battle against their fellow humans? Perhaps it is because nature can neither be disgraced nor dishonored. Courage may be proven without killing, as in the case of martyrdom, but whether passive or active witnesses are required to establish the ideological basis of the action. Cowardice is not willing to risk death by either aggression or militant submission.

If the self-interest of the person in the civil order is defined in purely economic terms, it is possible to generate the model of the self-disinterested person who does not care whether he or she survives or not (which is not to say that he or she wishes to die, i.e., to commit suicide). Total self-interest is intolerable because it subverts affiliation. If valor is the better part of discretion, it is the meaner part of affection. Total self-disinterest puts its incumbent beyond attachment because it presupposes indifference to life and death — but life must be valued in order to risk it. A person indifferent to life and death needs no stimulus like a flag, banner, medal, or even congratulations to face death. Therefore such a disposition is not accounted a virtue. Suicide is not honorable since the subject prefers not to live; it is not possible to sacrifice where there is nothing to sacrifice. Sacrifice is the giving up of something otherwise cherished. A god is unable to make a sacrifice because he or she is unable to suffer loss.

In the case of what has been recently called "non-violent" behavior, close examination discloses a paradoxically violent nexus — albeit a unilateral one. Nevertheless, the risk of violent death is the salient condition; for if it be absent — and the point is not intended to demean — the cadres who engage in passive resistance, the social matrix of non-violence, would lose their significance. The only condition under which one could imagine a literally "non-violent" encounter, at least from a sociological standpoint, would entail the confrontation of two non-violent groups which, in lieu of the militant objectives if these movements, would appear as nothing short of absurd.

Thus the fraternal ethos that systematically seeks the danger of violent, that is, premature death, whether in its bilateral or unilateral expression, includes the movements that yield only the appearance of the paradoxical designation "non-violent." The point may be vividly apprehended in the comments of Gandhi: "He who cannot protect himself or his nearest and dearest or their honor by non-violently facing death, may and ought to do so by violently dealing with an oppressor. He who can do neither is a burden." Indeed, the fraternal commitment to precipitate and honorific risk is so clearly predominant that aggressive violence, not civil compromise, remains for Gandhi the consistent alternative method: "I do believe that when there is a choice only between cowardice and violence, I would advise violence."

It will be perhaps rejoined that an odd sense of "conservation" and "social stucture" is being presented here. How can one compare the extensive civil structure and its long accumulated body of science, technology, commerce, and culture with the intensive fraternal structures that emerge only as transient episodes? As Burke puts it: "Rage and frenzy will pull down more in half an hour than prudence, deliberation and foresight can build up in a hundred years." This assertion, however, presumes that structure depends upon protracted duration and is denied to events whose outcomes appear as relatively brief or intermittent — a judgment that cannot pass close scrutiny.

The very notion of conservatism in the political domain is drawn from analogy to the mechanical conservation of energy which, though often misunderstood by political writers, is given to an unwitting vitalism not inconsistent with the organic model of successive adaptation of varying forms. As Burke rightly asserts: "A state without the means of some change is without the means of its conservation." Accordingly, he elaborates:

> The British constitution has not been struck out in heat by a set of presumptuous men, like the assembly of pettifoggers run mad in Paris. "Tis not the hasty product of a day, but the well ripened fruit of wise delay." It is the result of the thoughts of many minds in many ages. It is no simple, no superficial thing, nor to be estimated by superficial understandings. An ignorant man, who is not fool enough to meddle with his clock, is, however sufficiently confident to think that he can safely take to pieces and put together at his pleasure, a moral machine of another guise, importance, and complexity composed of far other springs and balances and counteracting and cooperating powers.

In the clockwork analogy with an orderly society, once the mechanism is precipitately taken apart, all elements are released to an "unconnected chaos."

For the sake of argument, let us accept Burke's analogy to the clock. It takes a certain effort to coil up a clock's spring to overcome its resistant elastic force. The coiled spring now possesses the acquired force or potential energy to drive the mechanism through a cycle of incrementally fine movements that appear to the eye as the gradually altered positions of the hands on the face of the time piece.

Now if taken by presumption someone should pry open the clock and break the controlling escapement ratchet, the stored energy would be precipitately released; and this release could be described as violent. In any event, the sudden and concentrated discharge decidedly does not express an "unnatural" generation of some undesirable quantity of energy, nor can it be referred outside of time to a suspended "void." By contrast to the gradual change of state, the more violent expenditure represents a different, albeit intensified, mode of distributing the reserve of force. Neither the moderate nor the violent release represent a static or chaotic movement, but differentiated time rates of change.

If we examine the question of violence in the most disinterested terms, we associate its expression with a sudden discharge of augmented and compressed force that might have otherwise been inhibited by forbearance or alternatively exhibited by a gradual expenditure, and hence attenuation of potential effort. It is therefore to be observed that violence is predicated on a certain alternative distribution of available energy. A given reserve of force can be rapidly exhausted by the precipitate, concentrated impact of a closed fist or alternatively gradually dissipated in friction by more gentle ministration, the more judicious parcelling out of effort expended by an open handed massage. But at the extreme, the violent gesture constitutes the greatest possible exertion the agent can muster at a given moment with available muscular force in the shortest possible time (at the optimum velocity) against a given target. This effort may be efficiently augmented by the mechanical advantage of 1) a weapon and 2) by joining forces with other like-minded individuals; gaining strength through combination.

A process is thus denoted as violent when its expression is intense but brief as contrasted with an alternate displacement of the given available energy when the expression of effort is protracted but attenuated. An example would be the alternative effort of the engaged constituents to persist in an indefinitely longer period of contiguous interaction.

All we are able to say at this point is that violent expression is a generic alternative as it connotes a brief but intense expenditure of effort as opposed to the less violent or more gentle expenditure of effort. Other examples drawn from commonplace experience may shed light on this problem. The act of the violinist deftly performing a staccato passage upon his instrument, peremptorily cutting short the duration of tone in the process, may be contrasted in its violence with the protracted tone evoked by continuous bowing, legato-style. But we should hardly be persuasive for all that if we argued that the precipitately brief staccato passages or violent plucking represented a void in the composition.

Analogously, our phonetic expressions of the consonants "p" and "b" are designated as "plosives" because they require a sudden and intense expiration of breath, and they in turn may be contrasted in their violence with the "fricatives," e.gs., "s," "th," marked by the slower sustained expiration. But we should not win a serious audience if we insisted that our vocal organs were convulsively dissolved when we chose to utter "push" instead of "thrush."

If we are disposed to avoid the inordinate damage the intense exertion entails, we shall wish to exhaust all intermediate opportunities and assume as our standard the motto Louis XIV ironically inscribed upon his cannons: Ultima Ratio Regium — the last resort of kingship. Alternatively, if a constituency is stymied by the graduated and attenuated processes of civil interaction requiring the release from the unendurable pressure of the established regime, the cry of the syndicalist would seem apt: "One hour of revolutionary violence is worth twenty years of parliamentary chatter."

But whether viewed as a last resort from the civil vantage or as a precipitate *first step* from the fraternal standpoint, violent action is conceived as an abrupt departure from a prior set of gradually ordered moves. It represents a generic disruption of the repertoire of specialized human activities drawing all the diverse components of the division of labor, actually or potentially, into the monolithic momentum of the struggle, either as combatants or as auxiliaries on the "home front." By this I mean the extensively ordered civil society converted into a "nation-in-arms," whether directed against itself in the divided form of two fraternal factions during civil war, or against an integral fraternal counterpart during foreign war. These periods of intensive affiliation are conceived as brief and intermittent, bracketed parenthetically in such cases as 1914-1918, 1939-1945. Where we compute civil history in the relatively nondescript terms of centuries or epochs, we place revolution and war in exemplary temporal categories of days and months.

Yet however brief, they are marked off with special periodicity as the watershed moments of intensive change: July 4, 1776; July 14, 1789; September 1, 1939; December 7, 1941; days commemorated for their fame or infamy, but in any case selected out from the extensive succession of otherwise relatively anonymous and unheralded days of attenuated civil routine. In this sense, the intensive intervals literally become the eponymous days or months. The days or months with especially dated or named significance stand in contrast with *anonymous* days lost, without name, to historic memory precisely because they are unexceptional in the day-to-day regularity of the contained antagonism of *la vie quotidienne*.

Under the intensive pressure of such denominations as les journées the system fixing the division of civil time, the calendar itself, is radically superseded or altered. It is sufficient to recall the displacement of the Julian calendar by the French and Russian revolutionaries. Certainly, these extensive civil orderings and intensive fraternal orderings of time offer mutually exclusive liabilities and are alternately choiceworthy to the historic membership, depending upon the nature of institutional commitments and the exigencies of the particular context.

At this point, it may be appropriate to exemplify the alternate evaluations of civil and fraternal structure with regard to the intensive process. On the civil side of the ledger there is Cicero's famous declaration:

> However highly Themistocles ... may be extolled — and deservedly, and however much Salamis may be cited as witness of his most glorious victory — a victory glorified above Solon's statesmanship in instituting the Areopagus — yet Solon's achievement is not to be accounted less illustrious than his. For Themistocles' victory served the state *once and only once*; while Solon's work will be of service *forever*. For through his legislation, the laws of the Athenians and the institutions of their father are maintained. (*De Officiis*, I, 22.75. My italics.)

But taken from the fraternal side, there is Shakespeare's *Henry V* urging on his troops prior to the battle of Agincourt by appeal to the magnified value of the keenly joined risk about to be undertaken on that singular day:

> This day is called the feast of Crispin.
> He that outlives this day and comes safe home
> Will stand a-tiptoe when this day is named
> And rouse him at the name of Crispin ...
> Then he will strip his sleeve and show his scars,
> And say "these wounds I had on Crispin's Day."
> And ... from this day to the ending of the world,
> But we in it shall be remembered —
> We few, we happy few, we band of brothers.
> For he today that sheds his blood with me
> Shall be my brother, Be he ne'er so vile,
> This day shall gentle his condition.
> He then, by contrast, offers the unexalted
> Picture of civil security, figured as the
> "Gentlemen in England now abed" who
> Shall think themselves accursed they were not here,
> And hold their manhoods cheap while any speaks
> That fought with us upon Saint Crispin's Day.
> (Act IV, Scene 3)

I have tried to show that the intensive interval of violence is construed on the traditional view as a structural intermission in the otherwise extended but attenuated processes of civil succession marked by limited antagonism and hence by pursuit of incremental advantages — superseded in turn by further accumulation on the individual's heightened schedule of expectations. One's most recent achievement at any level is immediately conjoined to relative dissatisfaction by reference to the foreseeable maximum, prompting again an extended effort at acquisition and renewed sufferance. We appropriately call this condition of continuously augmented but indefinitely resolved effort within the civil order that is free of disjunctive violence, civil success.

If the problem of violence assumes an anomalous position in our temporal categories, it fits poorly with the bounded spatial configuration we ascribe to civil life, that is, the container convention representing the area of civil conduct by orientation to circumventing walls or demarcated locations, and to the bounded embrace of the laws. I have correspondingly noted that in complement the process of violence is conceived as constitutionally exogenous to the domicile, but sanctioned only on the *terra incognita* or under the collapse of the contained location in civil insurrection or foreign invasion executed outside the law in the void, the structural interregnum attendant upon the "desolating barricades" of the ruined civil environs.

These sites of unfettered battle under the constraint of "continual fear and danger of violent death" do not allow a space for industry, commerce, or culture, and traditional diurnal occupations. Yet it is evident that these "no-man's lands," where nothing but death is produced when the day's "work" is done, become commemorated as sacred landmarks, sacralized precisely by the risk, if not sufferance of violent death. "And those that leave their valiant bones in France, dying like men, though buried in your dunghills, they shall be famed." Yet before the precipitate struggle the terrain remained undistinguished and comparatively unremarked by the larger constellation of citizenry.

Of what significance to the Greek citizenry was Marathon or the narrow pass at Thermopylae prior to the battle waged there; or the nondescript field at Zama to the Romans before Scipio defeated Hannibal there; or Pharsalia before the fratricidal civil war executed in its precincts? What recognition did the place name "Waterloo" evoke to English, French or Belgians prior to the contest, or, in advance of the civil and foreign engagements, Gettysburg, the Ardennes forest, and Iwo Jima to the Americans? After the battle, however, they assume overnight a codistinctive status with the civil sanctuary itself. Far from remaining anonymous vacuis locis, they become inextricably linked with the civic centers themselves: barren battlefields, domestic or foreign, join the long standing sites of accumulated civilization as handmaidens to historic memory and marked with monuments both at home and abroad. They are the interstitial location of transient communities, the fraternal proving ground where nothing is constructed but much is sacrificed.

VIOLENCE AND SOCIALITY

(1974-1975)

The problem of violence engages social inquiry on fundamental terms, but it is, for all that, not easy to compose as a social problem. It needs only to be considered that the very notion of a social boundary is based on the limitation of expressed antagonism. By definition, to do violence means to exceed this limit; hence, its outbreak is unavoidably viewed as outside or discontinuous with social form. At the extreme, the manifestation of violence, in Hobbes' oft quoted words, leaves in the breach: "No place for industry, no culture on the earth, no knowledge on the face of the earth; no account of time; no arts; no letters; no society — and worst of all, continual fear of danger and violent death; the life of man solitary, poor, nasty, brutish and short."[1] In the same way, Edmund Burke speaks to the revolutionary break in France's historic order as "an unsocial, uncivil, unconnected chaos."[2]

The violent interaction is viewed on these terms, by contrast with the forms of sustained and corrigible social activity, as an extinction of action — as ex-action; indicating a special intermission in the social process that cannot itself be compassed. It therefore yields the assumption, so to say, of null sociality.

This anomalous position of the problem of violence is not clarified, but reinforced by the view that conflict has a positive social value, giving way as a functional outlet for the otherwise bound constituents of a social structure. Simmel, whose work is most generally associated with this principle, is disposed to say that however extreme the consequences for the parties to it, the struggle conserves a socially constructive role even if it be increased, without hindrance, "to infinity."[3] This allows the unwelcome consequence that not only has no one in this annihilated world died in vain, but each and everyone has perished as a functional or therapeutic effect, for their own social good.

Such unresolved implications of this principle (which have a distinct edge in a nuclear age) surely taxed Simmel, for at other points in the discussion, he recoils from them, however inconsistently, by arguing that only limited dispute is functional. Thus he says that if the conflict is "wholly irrational and turbulent [and] the object of the conflict is suddenly eliminated [then] the whole movement swings into the void."[4] Here the most acute expression of human differences, if it "aims at annihilation"[5] does not enter the functional social picture at all — except as a "void" in the composition.

In order to circumvent the gravity of the issue, conflict is reduced, as it were, to sport; for the expressed differences between the parties, however severe, are only meaningfully disclosed if they are contained within predetermined limits. But the process of violence exceeds these limits and is therefore not an integral social phenomenon.

On the one hand, if violence becomes the multiplied consequence of a social conflict, then we have an inscrutable "void" where society ought to be. On the other hand, we can avert this difficulty by only treating of conflicts that do not seriously threaten the social order. But that is to beg the question. In either case, it will be evident that the problem of violence is returned to null sociality, for it cannot be coherently included in Simmel's notion of the social structure.

It is the same impulse in Freud that led him to oppose civilization to an arbitrary death instinct. But this idea represents a manifest contradiction of any comprehensible sense of "instinct," which for all its vagaries, assumes, at minimum, a vital function in recurrent service to a living organism. But if this be so, what then can be made of an "instinct" that precisely eliminates the condition of any instinct?[6] Thus, it seems that if the meaning of social order is made by exclusive contrast with the process of violence, the attempt to obtain the social context of the question inevitably yields anomalous results.

It is not accidental, but unavoidable, that as the problem becomes more critical it is ascribed to an explosive but untraceable medium of invisible pathologies, irrational death instincts, gratuitous gestures and epic spirits. This manner of proceeding is based on the assumption that intelligibility of social order diminishes as the process of violence is intensified.

In light of the foregoing we will briefly state the argument to follow. It will be shown that the range of alternatives that one ordinarily addresses on any significant question of social combination is, in the instance of violence, reduced to a rigid disjunction of terms: either civil society or elemental chaos. This distinction characteristically represents the civil form as a container that expels violence "outside" society to a criminal "underworld" or, on the other hand, to a *terra incognita* of foreign war. This containing form breaks down, however, under the impact of two general crises: domestic revolution or foreign invasion. For on these conditions the line dividing the safe enclosure from the removed dangers of the underworld or foreign battlefield is erased; hence, the uncontained chaos. But whether violence is discounted by relegation "outside" the container, or is viewed as collapsing in the general break-out of unpartitioned conflict, the issue is lost to inquiry. In the former because the question becomes marginal to the social constitution, and in the latter because it overwhelms its foundations in a "chaos total."

This line of difficulties leads us back to the brilliant formulation of Thomas Hobbes's *Leviathan*.

Hobbes had made the point, central to political thought, that society — whatever its size, economic organization or constitutional type — is founded and is conserved by the collective aversion to violence (and its unbound consequences). This aversion is expressed by a contractual readiness to restrain antagonism, to seek peace when others are willing, notwithstanding the difficulty the correspondents may have in reserving or dissimulating their spontaneous disposition on any particular occasion. Their mutual self-interest in physical security and external prosperity cannot but dictate all prudent effort in this direction.

To be sure, this convention does not exclude self-defense as a last resort, if all earnest attempts at reconciling differences or limiting the hostility have failed to yield what the convention is designed, after all, to insure: safety, if not in some state of ease, at least in some condition of tolerable improvisation. If one does not act in self-defense, and resigns oneself to the fatal outcome, one suffers immediately and, needless to say, abandons at once the condition of all civil effort and material acquisition. But fighting — back to the wall — holds out the possibility, however remote, of continued survival in the restored civil order. Hobbes rightly says of violence considered as the ultimo ratio: "If I do it not I die presently: If I do it, I die afterwards: And therefore by doing it, there is time of life gained: Nature therefore compels him to the fact."[7]

On the other hand, a provocative disregard for the peaceful opportunity, and an unbridled willingness to chance violence — not as a last but as a first resort — is a move that, by generalization, reduces the integrally governed civil body into a solitary, universal war of "every man against every man."[8] This condition, in the breach of civil association and lacking any external regulation, can be mitigated, at best, by tense and disoriented stalemates, fluctuating upon unaccountable individual whims.

The outcome of this argument is that we are presented with a strict conceptual choice between (1) a unique composition based on an agreement of mutual self-restraint in regard to violent means, qualified, to be sure, by the exigency of individual or corporate self-defense, or (2) a general decomposition of association when the corporate body is undone by provocative resort to violence. In other words, if the formal condition of social order requires, *sine qua non*, the collective aversion to violence, then on the contrary, the unqualified readiness to perpetuate and risk violent death can only give way to a convulsive chaos of that order.

It is thus understandable that the very principle of corporate form is visualized as a continuously ramified network of encompassing restraints that contain the unruly and aggrandizing disposition of the membership against a projected chaos of general war. The limitations on the members of the body politic, and their coordination in the interdependent operation of the division of labor, inhibit arbitrary antagonism even as they encourage a healthy rivalry of productive effort.

The conservation of the civil disposition presupposes that, however much the correspondents are covertly tempted to the immediate resolution of differences by violent means — by the duel — their enduring advantage rests on the side of confining behavior to at least restricted, if ramified, contests, to the bargaining process in the market or the dialogue in the framework of discourse. In this connection, we can perceive why civil order has characteristically taken the representation (however abstract the form) of a container — be it the embracing individual writ large, a ship of state, an enveloping sphere, a great Leviathan, an immense machine, or a social system.[9] However variously and picturesquely drawn, the exemplary works of political and social thought make visible the image of an architectonic vessel housing constituents "inside" a domain of safe recognizance, and expelling danger "outside," beyond the bourne, to a *terra incognita*, a raging sea, or a state of nature. In so far as the constituents have been brought under the enclosure, they secure, by convention of membership, a special if not unconditional immunity from violence — assuming they have not willingly placed themselves "outside" by reversion to aggressive conduct.

But men unite for the common safety to get themselves out of the universal danger of war and into the shelter of civil society. To that extent, hey require the constraint of sovereignty, or the legitimate monopoly of physical force as Weber defined the distinct means of the state for containing the social constitution.[10] Or as Hobbes had put the issue:

> "The final Cause, End, or Designe of men, in the introduction of that restraint upon themselves, is the foresight of their own preservation, and of a more contented life, thereby; that is to say of getting themselves out from that miserable condition of war, which is necessarily consequent to the natural Passion of men, when there is no visible power to keep them in awe, and tie them by fear of punishment to the performance of their covenants.[11]

If on this view the convergence of mutually binding agreements of self-restraint, whether explicit or tacit, provides only the necessary condition of social peace, the awe of the monopoly of force establishes the sufficient condition for its achievement. For "covenants without the sword are but words and of no strength to secure a man at all." One must recognize that this notion "the means of violence" includes the distinction as confused — both the available military ordinance at a given time, namely the technical imperative and the combatants commissioned as the ministerial "arm", to deploy the otherwise inert instruments on behalf of the established civil authority. And it is understood that these means — both the arms and the men — are used against domestic enemies defined outside the law, and against foreign enemies holding outside the territorial boundaries.

It will be evident from the preceding that civil society owns a structurally equivocal orientation to violence: if the condition *sine qua non* of the civil order is the abandonment of violent recourse by its putative constituents at the locus of refuge. The violent means are nonetheless sustained for the concentrated purpose of subduing the external enemies of the containing sanctuary. It follows that civil order cannot flourish with, or without, resort to violence. This equivocation is manifest in the concept "civil" itself. On the one hand, it is used to mean the very opposite of violent conduct; but on the other it is joined to it — as the civil-military *nexus*.

This equivocation rests in turn on the double sense of containment. If in this setting (of the political problem) the individual disposition to contain antagonism may be the rational reaction to the fear of violent death among human beings, considered as universal members of the species *qua species*, the social locus of containment is not at all coextensive with the species but militantly exclusive. It is self-evident that the body politic does not include the whole of mankind as its constituency. The political solution, is sub-contracted to a set of fractional associations that remain in a state of continuing belligerency.

Despite the insular image of the container, this situation implies that the state of nature is not, after all, left behind when men enter civil society, but is more precisely transposed "outside" to the foreign environment where the danger of violent death is immediately imposed by military obligation. It is manifest that the container can return its members to the "chaos" by "other means." But this is only to say that the members who enter upon the threshold of civil society do not, as one is inclined to suppose by reference to the container convention, open a door to get out of the arbitrary state of nature, and then irreversibly close it behind them at some boundary point in time or space. One should rather say that the constituents enter a revolving door which takes them — in peace and war, at home or on the foreign field — "in" and "out" of civil society by turns, without changing the constituents' direction. In the move for corporate safety the citizens are carried out to primordial danger without reversing course (just as the traveler of the tale, who sets out due east, unwittingly returns by circumnavigation to his point of origin without ever changing his direction).

What is left unexplained by this analysis is why the constituents are willing to immediately risk violent death on the foreign field when, by civil construction, the avoidance of that risk was the condition by convention of quitting the state of nature in the first place?

We shall, for the moment, pass by the significance of this equivocation and formulate it, unproblematically, in the following terms: the constitution of civil society does not eliminate the disposition to violence, but transposes the locus of its expression and concentrates the deposition of its authority. The role of armed force is, in other words, satisfied on behalf of civil order against human beings defined as external threats to the common safety of the domicile. The key problem of civil authority, then, is not the general elimination of violence, but the externalization of danger: 1) to foreign hosts assembled outside the territorial confines; 2) to criminals and revolutionaries defined outside the law representing, as it were positions "beyond" or "below" the enclosure of society; inhabiting the "underworld" or "underground."

What is decisive here is that much civil authority internally monopolizes the means of violence (considered as the inert instrument of deterrence), but the actual use of violence is characteristically transposed "outside" society proper. The violent engagement, for all its awesome consequences, is by necessary fiction visualized beyond the container of the established refuge. Even if the civil-criminal opposition assumes that crime is committed within the sovereign boundaries, within the physical confines of the political order, the act is represented as outside its encompassing law. If the civil-military nexus, on the other hand, authorizes the armed forces to do violence outside the bounding walls of the sanctuary — upon the no-man's land of just war — its mission is accounted as *within the law*. However contrary their ascribed legal values, these acts of violence are characterized as *external to the domain of civil order*. The acts of aggression are not conceived as indigenous, but exotic to the refuge.

By means of this two-fold separation of violence — alienated on the one side at a benign legal distance as deviant and hence extraordinary acts, or exported, on the other side, as removed acts of war at a magnified territorial distance — that society takes the form of an exclusive sanctuary, hedging in the disposition of the membership by reference to the corporate objectives of security and enterprise, ready to fortify these objectives by the employment of the police and expeditionary forces. But two general crises of the civil association that manifestly indicate the failure of its containing order to expel violence outside the legal margins by the threat of judicial punishment, or up to or beyond the defensible territorial perimeter by the martial discipline of the armed forces. Not necessarily exclusive events, these are domestic insurrection and external invasion. One or the other, or both, represent a breakdown of the delineating boundary between sanctuary and locus of conflict. They represent the breach of the sacred boundary the Romans set between the *domi et militiae*, the home and the field; only the most notorious transgression recorded as the crossing of the Rubicon by Caesar's armies. But whether conceived as originating from the direction of the domicile as insurrection, or referred to the field as invasion, these vicissitudes reduce the boundary separating the privileged locus of civil negotiation and the ruinous field of alien battle to an uncontained frontier of disorder, when viewed, that is, from the framework of the civil fraction itself. As the sanctuary and the no-man's land become indivisibly confounded, so do the civil-criminal and civil-military jurisdictions based on them collapse upon each other. On what ground, then, can the legal authority separate out violent dispositions as both criminal and honorable: What can the meaning of "inside" or "outside", by orientation to a containing tranquillity and an external danger, be when the boundary between them has been effaced?

If violent disposition cannot be externalized to the battlefield, or harnessed as a functional "means" to civil purpose in the massive breach of the authoritative locus — if the aggression cannot be held down to a manageable deviation, to tolerable frequency by the awe of sovereign order — then the readiness for violence itself becomes normative in the community. Insurrection generalizes the effects of crime beyond the underworld, as invasion generalizes the effects of war beyond the battlefield. This is only to say that civil terms dividing out violence as deviant criminality — removed from acts of war — are deprived of sensible correspondence by the gravest events that belie them. The conditions of revolution and invasion impart the violent breach of these same norms that otherwise either contain or distribute violence as marginal crime and external combat.

One is at a loss to explain these critical events by reference to the civil order they collapse. Requirements of general inquiry into violence are always greater than the level of analysis licensed by the container convention and systematically excluded by the contracted bounds of civil association (both as a set of secular constraints and as a threshold for theoretical consideration). Nor is it accidental that we are advised there is nothing evident in the breach but a "void in society" or a decomposition of social structure into an indiscriminate "war of everybody against everybody!"

The breakdown of the container allows no coherent social alternative in the breach — only abrupt dissolution. The rupture appears too confounding for comprehension other than an identification of violence with null sociality: "No culture on earth — no knowledge on the face of the earth; no account of time; no arts; no letters; no society." The question is abandoned precisely when it becomes most serious. We face the brittle disjunction of the available terms: the bound civil order, expelling violence beyond its enclosed boundaries, or a precipitate collapse and boundless disorder — a container or a chaos. Either the problem is "outside" the social order, or the social order is nullified. Violence is contained, functionally discounted to the margin by the incorporated members; or unconfined and incomprehensible. In any case, the question has been lost to inquiry — the context of social activity has been denied.

We attribute a unique and self-sufficient composition to civil society — including the members safely inside — by making violence a ministerial instrument without segregating the issue beyond the bourne. We are immediately delivered by the range of our terms to deny a coherent structure and assert a chaotic dissolution of the social connection on the occasion of its violent upheaval. We are forced to make a choice between a fixed container and an unlimited chaos — between a unique solution and unique dissolution of affiliation — without understanding the ground of this metaphoric disjunction in the first place.

We both exaggerate the social connection and, alternately, the limitless chaos of social form considered as coexisting members in a body politic. We correspondingly exaggerate the continuous succession of civil order through historical time. We can view the violent contretemps only as a structural intermission in an otherwise indivisible social continuum. In other words, if the container convention misinforms our understanding of the social problem by reference to a certain model of corporate place, it no less misinforms our orientation to time.

Edmund Burke, contemplating the French revolution, believed that the constitution of society, transmitted in "unbroken unity through all the ages," was then at hazard.[12] "The whole chain and continuity of the commonwealth would be broken; no one generation could link with the other; men would become little better than the flies of summer."[13] In consequence, he accounts, the "primeval contract of external society" gives way to an "unsocial, uncivil, unconnected chaos,"[14] and a "void in society."[15] We are beset when we give inquiry to the violent breach of the ancient regime by an anomalously interposed time out of historic time. But let us follow out Burke's reasoning if only for the sake of clarifying the difficulty we have here. We should ask how it is that the disconnected constituents drawn into the historic vacuum, the "void in society," survive this lapse of social structure to resume the historic process, *ex nihilo,* as an incorporate society. Chain and continuity of commonwealth is broken at the annihilating intermission, depriving the one generation of linkage with the next, so we shall not know how to make sense of the gap between predecessor and successor regimes. We have no choice but to follow the uninterrupted historic continuum to the point of violent exit — at the break make a fiat leap over the imponderable gap to an arbitrary point of reentry, given suddenly as the new regime. Is the great chain of society still a chain if its critical links are missing? If we gainsay these decisive turning points into an "unconnected chaos," are we then to harness our discipline to the theodicity of alternating constitutions between intermittent voids? Are we then brought to the paradox: the *urbs aeternas* never dies, but nonetheless suffers periodic annihilation? It will be evident that if we cannot describe these gaps but by argument to the chaos, then we will not be able to understand the historic transformations achieved through a given society during the violent interim. If our concept of social order is unintelligibly set off against the process of violence, can we even hope to comprehend either the order or change of social form?

No one can sensibly deny that civil society and its attendant culture falls out to grave disarray in the circumstances contemplated by Hobbes and Burke. But to assume from the demonstrable breach of civil order that social affiliation is categorically exhausted in a chaos of its elements, or that it leaves but an irreducible intermission in the social process, is to beg the question we must immediately take up. If we hold that the social constitution makes coherent sense only by exclusive contrast with a state of boundless violence, then we shall not, after a moment, be able to discover the ground for discussion. Even as we begin an earnest search, we have already set the issue beyond the negotiable range of inquiry. If violence cannot be maintained as an instrument to the strategic objectives of civil authority, we warrant that, in the breach, chaos has been let loose on the whole order of society. Correspondingly, if we cannot impute self-interested motives to individuals who initiate violent actions in reckless disregard of consequences, we allow that the action is arbitrary or senseless.

Whether our inquiry is taken up to the synthesis of the social complex, or taken down to the intelligibility of individual motives, the construction is confounded. We may raise this bafflement of motive to a principle and call it a death-instinct, or ascribe it, in Sorel's mythic terms, to an "epic-consciousness,"[16] to an *élan révolutionnaire febrile*, but we shall not be able to relate individuals to their social context in the absence of a formal principle of composition.. We are disposed to refer the question back to is context and inquire: (1) Is social form conserved in the vicissitudes of violence despite the manifest disorder of civil society? and (2) What is the nature of this social form? We shall discover some obvious proportion to these questions.

What we recognize under the impact of civil or foreign conflict is not, after all, an atomizing and indiscriminate war of everybody against everybody, but a determined division into closely bound sides; a division — in the suspension of civil relations — that forces the imperative choice of affiliation, that places constituents in the solitary position of joining — unequivocally — one side or the other. Far from atomizing all connections in the breach, the outbreak of violence — as it is concomitant of "taking sides" — intensifies affiliation beyond the expected degree of civil interaction. Civil interaction requires the limitation of both antagonism and affiliation if expectations of custodial order and productive rivalry are to be met.

Whatever the scale of collective violence, it is characteristically sided by a call for a demonstration of unqualified affiliation otherwise prudently ruled out in the confines of civil negotiation. Let the sides by gangs (Alphas vs. Betas), or revolutionary divisions (North vs. South, Red vs. White), or nations combined to wage a world wear (Axis vs. Allies). Whatever the scale or justification, the threshold of adversarial violence could not be reached if it only brought forth an atomized and chaotic multitude. We do not discover a formless upheaval of the elements at these moments, but a consolidation of social force by division into strictly opposing lines, typically represented by the following oath: "On 6 and 10 Pluviose, Year II, the *Société de sans-culottes révolutionaires* swore the most intimate union and fraternity and declared eternal hatred towards anyone who would dare separate them."[17] The panic of dissolving ranks presupposes a previous state of morale — a shared and heightened readiness to risk the prime danger, a commitment made by contrast with the prudential constraints of civil association.

Taken on these terms, the container convention fails to adequately account for: (1) how the process of violence goes to *coherence* sides and not to an elementary *chaos*, and (2) why individuals, otherwise pursuing a closely husbanded self-interest, precipitately put their life at risk in the company of their peers when, by all civil measure, men shun violent death by "an impulsion of nature, no less than that whereby a stone moves downward."

It is noteworthy in this connection that David Hume, after reviewing the principle of association based on the coincidence of self-interests, found it unaccountable that "men in respect of factions often very violent should attach themselves so very strongly to persons with whom they are nowise acquainted, whom perhaps they never saw, and from whom they never received nor can hope any favor: yet this we often find to be the case, and even with men who, on other occasions discover no great generosity of spirit nor are easily found to be transported by friendship beyond their own interest."[18]

If we cannot accept the convention of null sociality there must be a social force sufficient to suspend the ground of self-interested values, to overcome the fear of violent death — however inconsistent this disposition appears to the claim of civil order that the ultimate basis of sociality is the constituents' continuing safety and commodious augmentation of interest. However various the social manifestations — criminal factions (juvenile and adult), revolutionary unions, commissioned armies defending the territory or invading another on imperial expedition — these combinations possess, below their salient differences of justification, a common underlying form that depends on the break with, or physical separation from, civil order. This further implies — absenting the container — that they present their members with the immediate prospect of irrevocable danger as a condition of membership.

We shall recognize then that the division of social order into militant sides conserves an alternate affiliation in the breach of civil association: if the aversion to violent death conserves civil order, the risk of violent death conserves fraternal order. Affiliation under the impact of violence then is conserved through a fundamental change in the form of affiliation. What is implied by this formulation is that civil society is not the general but the limiting case of association. It is not a question of civil society, or null sociality, but of two distinguishable levels of social incorporation — one based on the aversion to, the other involving by commitment to the hazard of imminent danger. From the standpoint of a given constituent, these alternatives of association exert differential pressure. The problem of violence cannot be understood as the received distinction between conservatives and radicals, between a force, inveterately holding the social constitution together, and extremists threatening to dissipate it by violent challenge. It is not a question of conserving or dissipating, whatever our ethical compunctions. Both aversion to, and the provocation of, violence conserve affiliation — given that one is sustained by limiting the outer range of the other. If societies go from one regime state to another by the process of collective violence — however different their ideology at the beginning or end of the process — whether the old regime is restored or the innovative ideology succeeds, the social structure does not dissolve or emerge from a void. It is transformed into the fraternal form by division into irreconcilable sides.

The fraternal permutation applies to radical change in the same society, translated through civil war. It also applies to the violent displacement of sovereign regimes coexisting at the same period — conquest by foreign war. What characterizes this transformation of social order is not an exclusive problem of the disjunctive succession of regime forms — from aristocratic to democratic franchise. This passage could be made only on the condition that in the interim, when stable authority is itself being contested, there had already occurred a transformation from civil to fraternal order, which we otherwise are wont to dismiss as the "uncivil, unsocial, unconnected chaos."

Surely it can be argued that these transient episodes of fraternal incorporation — war or revolution, or violence at the margins of society — cannot be viewed as *owning* integral composition. We are inclined to think that the brevity of these "moments" denies elaboration of social structure that we ordinarily associate with long and arduously cultivated bodies of science, industry and commerce disrupted by these sudden tempests. This attitude wrongly assumes that the significance of the upshot can be measured by its duration. On the contrary, the intensity and weight of the fraternal affiliation is intimately bound up with the risk of precipitate loss — the time compression of commitment we cannot avoid viewing as *interstitial to civil life*.

When wars are prolonged for years, we bracket them out of civil history, such as 1914-1918 and 1939-1945. These periods are conceived of as breaks in time. During the French and Russian revolutions the civil calendar was superseded to suit both the exalted position and the fateful compression of these events by a revolutionary reckoning of time.[19] The interstitial position of fraternal order is associated most especially with the days: *Les journées*, the May days, the June days, the July days, "the ten days that shook the world," July 4, July 14. One may hold with the vision of Burke that these turning points "pull down more in half an hour than prudence, deliberation and foresight can build up in a hundred years"; or one may echo the syndicalist cry: "One hour of revolution is worth twenty years of parliamentary chatter."

Whether viewed as a last step from the vantage of civil defense, or as the militant first move of fraternal cohorts, mobilization represents an abrupt departure from a prior set of ordered social moves — a generic disruption of the repertoire of specialized human activities. Mobilization draws all the variegated components of the division of labor into the monolithic momentum of the struggle as combatants or auxiliaries "on the home front". Civil society is converted into a "nation in arms". These moments cannot be estimated by the brevity of their duration to civil chronology. They risk being viewed as chaotic gaps in the pre-existing civil structure, or as anomalous intermissions in the historical process.

If the intensive fraternal process assumes a problematic, exemplary position in ones temporal perspective, so do the spatial loci of the precipitate struggle — the no-man's land — by reference to the bounded and ramified identity of the civil metropolis. Otherwise anonymous, these sites assume eponymous status overnight (What recognition did the place-name "Waterloo" evoke to either the French or the English prior to the engagement?) After the struggle, these non-descript precincts become irreversibly associated with the civic centers themselves. Barren battlefields, domestic or foreign, join the long-standing centers of accumulated civilizations in co-association: consecrated as the location of transitory communities, the fraternal ground where nothing is constructed, but where much is sacrificed.

Why is civil order vulnerable to the call for fraternal demonstration of affiliation when that call challenges the existence of its members? The Hobbesian assumption is that the condition of society obliges constituents to restrain their spontaneous, unreflected disposition if the population is to survive as an association. If everyone expressed their attitudes with unmitigated intensity, the system could not contain the consequences. If all individuals had their thoughts and impressions spontaneously published on their foreheads, chances are high that each meeting between correspondents would be the last meeting — the dissolution of society into a state of war. A parallel of immediate impressions (states of nature) and public expressions (states of society) is unsupportable. The price of security is duplicity. Social unity is possible only through the duplicity of its correspondence. One is obliged to dissimulate one's antipathy toward others to achieve stable accommodation and augment one's relative position.

To argue that unqualified veracity would invite war of unlimited antagonism is not to say that civil society could survive by unconditional duplicity. If everyone misrepresented their state of mind on every occasion of correspondence, no one could be trusted. The minimal condition of exchange would be erased.

What characterizes civil exchange, if not an unqualified deliverance of experience, is the prudent return for dissimulating the state of things holding on some, if not all occasions. Its order is based on an endemic indeterminacy between the veracity and duplicity of representation. The problem did not escape Adam Smith:

> How is it possible to ascertain by rules the exact point at which, in every case, a delicate sense of justice begins to run into a frivolous and weak scrupulousness of conscience? When it is that secrecy and reserve begin to grow into dissimulation?[20]

What permits negotiation through this indeterminate state of affairs is the mutual interest each party has in choosing to give the benefit to the other. It is not the liability of the doubt, assuming in any case a civil remedy is available for breach of contract. Common safety and the advance of material interests is based on the assumption that constituents will refrain from challenging each other's prudent appearances based on mutually agreed self-restraint. To unconditionally challenge this duplicity — to give the lie to appearances — is to signal reversion to the condition of open antagonism. It will subvert the stability and predictability of any civil order based on containment of provocation. But if civil membership dictates some indeterminate level of misrepresentation of others for the sake of safety, no one can escape self-misrepresentation, hence self-doubt, to whatever extent one views oneself as a member of a civil society. If the price of security is duplicity, the cost of duplicity as the liability of civil life is uncertainty about where people stand in regard for one another. This uncertainty, and the need to discover the ground level of association, is the chronic problem of civil order. At critical moments there is pressure to force the issue. The problem is to demonstrate the basic, final state of affiliation in a system that puts a premium on misrepresenting the level of association achieved by the container convention.

Civil relations carry implicit demands for proof. A demonstration is called out in the crises of civil relations to manifest what is in doubt — the genuineness of commitment. No formal demonstration in discourse can serve this purpose. No linguistic procedure exists for establishing the veracity or duplicity of assurance on matters when language itself is the problematic conveyance of self-interest. The demonstration of affiliation is achieved by a move that cannot be dissimulated, the risk *sine qua non* of self-interested values and symbolic exchange — of life itself in the presence of one's peers.

Thus a situation issue, by provocation or defense, in which affections and disaffection are evinced unequivocally by the sides chosen and the mutual exchange of risks. Lives are put in danger, one for the other, demonstrating the fidelity of the relation by unconditional sacrifice one is prepared to make and receive reciprocally for it. The nexus based on the risk exchange — not on incremental capital risk but the unlimited fatal risk — is made even more critical by those who unequivocally declare in opposition as enemies: declared on the ground of irreconcilable differences that cannot be negotiated by civil means, but only settled by recourse to arms.

The proof of affiliation by way of the precipitate process of violence resolves the indeterminacy of amity and enmity by forcing an unequivocal disjunction of affiliation. Civil competition is based on the limitation of affiliation and antagonism in order to produce unfettered exploitation of opportunities and limit the liability of irreversible investment. Civil life provides a contingent means for the rational elaboration of mutual self-interest, but it cannot provide the basis for an ultimate assurance of unqualified association.

In summary, the imposition and risk of violence constitutes a reciprocal demonstration of affiliation in lieu of the indeterminate ground of civil interaction.[21] The underlying issues can be drawn more directly by reconsideration of Freud's notion of the "death-instinct" analyzed in the context of the container convention.

Freud wrote that "the natural instinct of aggressiveness in man, the hostility of each one against all and of all against each one, opposes the program of civilization."[22] He is paraphrasing Hobbes' version of the state of nature, agreeing that the natural condition of man — set in contrast with the effort of civil containment — is expressed in atomized war of everybody against everybody. Freud ascribes this condition to an innate, independent instinctual disposition in people. He admitted that he found it elusive in any notion of a physiological mechanism.[23] This irreducible death instinct, as a clinical concept, like Hobbes' primordial chaos, needs to be examined in the light of the questions raised in the opening discussion. The risk of death in fraternal conformation is posed to obtain the benefits of surviving a danger, having proved one's mettle, and meriting, after the fact, the social commendation of escutcheon and medal. The members of the cohort are not driven on as if compelled by an inveterate longing for their own particular destruction, but by a disposition to prove they are not afraid to risk the possibility, otherwise terror-striking, in order to win the unconditional approbation of their oath-bound comrades.

Consider the following recollection of an initiate to a gang war:

> I was in a chill sweat over being shot or cut up. However, when the battle cry "Bishops going down" sounded, I piled out with the rest. I was scared to go to battle, but more scared to deuce out in front of my club.[24]

In a different context, in his historic *Essay on Crimes and Punishments*, Beccaria raises the question of the duel:

> In vain have the [civil] laws endeavored to abolish this custom by punishing the offenders with death. A man deprived of the esteem of others, foresees that he must be reduced either to a solitary existence, insupportable to social creatures, or become the object of perpetual insult; consideration sufficient to overcome the fear of death.[25]

The limitation of antagonism, which is indispensable to civil order, is viewed in honor-bound company as the generic absence of commitment — cowardice. The fear of social isolation forces the precipitate hazard upon the members — the duel. The mutual risk of violence, viewed as consolidation of affiliation, does not signal chaotic dissolution, the null sociality, or the outbreak of autonomous death-instincts, but the transformation of social form based on limited liability of social contract — the unconditional affiliation of the militant oath: "Amongst a free people, there are no uncommitted citizens — there are only brothers and enemies."[26] It is not that the body politic dissolves into the chaotic multitude but that basis of membership is no longer assumed. One needs to prove membership by precipitate action, to prove that one's verbal promises *against* self-interest are credible — when by any civil measure the contrary conduct is expected. At the fraternal moment, society produces loyalty by demanding the reversal of what otherwise is considered prudent conduct.[27] The indeterminacy of representation is no longer given the benefit but the liability of the doubt. One must now stand up and be counted. One must swear the oath to test the veracity and finality of one's allegiance. This involves transformation from a civil to a fraternal sociality.

The process of purging civil society of the duplicity of contingent attachment leaves in the breach no other choice than unconditional union. The alternative is unconditional isolation. In the absence of the civil gradient of choice, the break from civil association to reach indivisible union sets up radical oscillation between morale and panic, sublimity and terror.

In a nuclear age the issue of fraternal process raises the question of risk to a new level. The need to prove beyond reasonable doubt that humans are capable of unqualified association endangers human life altogether. Civil disposition, called in with increasing refinement of technology to deal with social life as a matter of its appearance and not of its substance, produces the uneasiness to transform sociality again by an ultimate test. This has been a critical question posed in the last generation — a generation that questioned what it was that really bonded society.

NOTES

1. The *English Works of Thomas Hobbes*, ed. William Molesworth (London: John Bohn, 1839), III, 113.
2. *The Writings and Speeches of Edmund Burke* (Beaconsfield Edition; New York: J. F. Taylor, 1901), III, 360.
3. *Conflict and the Web of Group-Affiliations*, trans. Kurt H. Wolff and Reinhard Bendix (New York: The Free Press, 1964), p. 25.
4. Ibid., p. 112.
5. Ibid., p. 26.
6. *The Ego and the Id*, trans. Joan Rivière (New York: W. W. Norton, 1960), chap. iv. *Civilization and Its Discontents*, trans. Joan Rivière (London: Hogarth Press, 1951), chap. vi.
7. Hobbes, Vol. III, p. 288.
8. Hobbes, Vol. III, p. 115.
9. As modern examples of the disjunction between the container and the chaos we may first cite Adam Smith in his *The Theory of Moral Sentiments*:

> "Human society, when we contemplate it in a certain abstract and philosophic light appears like a great, and immense machine, whose regular and harmonious movements produce a thousand agreeable effects. As in any other beautiful and noble machine that was the production of human art, whatever tended to render its movements more smooth and easy would derive a beauty from this effect, and on the contrary, whatever tended to obstruct them would displease upon that account...."

Smith later quotes the author of the *Leviathan* to support the view that, antecedent to the containing machine of civil government, "there could be no safe and peaceable society among men. To preserve society was to support civil government, and to destroy civil government was the same thing as to put an end to society." (*Adam Smith's Moral and Political Philosophy*, ed. Herbert W. Schneider [New York: Hafner, 1948], pp. 52-54).

Another straightforward example of this orientation derives from a commentary by Emile Durkheim:

> "By an altogether artificial coercion, [the state] can, for a time, hold in check all the internal contradictions, all the destructive conflicts which beset the society, but sooner or later these will tear it asunder .... The state of war which society conceals in its bosom must someday come to ahead, bringing with it the natural consequences, namely, the breaking of all social bonds and the decomposition of the social body" (quoted in Steven Lukes, *Emile Durkheim* [New York: Harper and Row], 1972. See also *The Division of Labor in Society,* trans. George Simpson (New York: Free Press, 1964] p. 360; pp. 392-395).

"It is possible to define the 'political' character of a corporate group only in terms of the means peculiar to it, the use of force. This means is, however . . . indispensable to its character. It is even, under certain circumstances, elevated into an end itself." (*The Theory of Social and Economic Organization*, trans. A. M. Henderson and Talcott Parsons [New York: Oxford, 1947], p. 155).

11. Hobbes, Vol. III, p. 153.
12. Burke, Vol. III, p. 263.
13. Ibid., p. 357.
14. Ibid., p. 360.
15. Ibid., p. 46.
16. *Réflexions sur la violence* (Paris: Marcel Riviére, 1946), p. 388.
17. Albert Soboul, *The Parisian Sans-Culottes and the French Revolution: 1793-4* (Oxford: Clarendon Press, 1964), p. 157.
18. *Essays: Moral, Political, and Literary*, Ed. T. H. Green and T. H. Grose (London: Longmans, Green, 1898), I, 133.
19. For an analysis of the Republican calendar instituted by decree in October of 1793, see Pierre Caron, *Manuel pratique pour L'étude de la révolution française* (Paris: 1947), pp. 281-287.
20. Smith, p. 66
21. Thus, Adam Smith avers in the *Theory of Moral Sentiments*:

"Society may subsist among men, as among different merchants, from a sense of utility, without any mutual love or affection; and though no man in it should owe any obligation, or be bound in gratitude to any other, it may still be upheld by a mercenary exchange of goods according to an agreed valuation."

At the same time he recognizes the tax on fellowship that the market imposes on its correspondents:

"In civilized society he stands at all times in the need of the cooperation and assistance of great multitudes, while his whole life is scarce sufficient to gain the friendship of a few persons." (*The Wealth of Nations*, ed. J. R. McCulloch [Edinburgh: A. and C. Black, and W. Tait, 1838], Bk. I, ch. ii, p. 7).

22. Freud, *Civilization and Its Discontents*, p. 102.
23. Freud, *The Ego and the Id*, p. 32.
24. Ira Henry Freeman, *Out of the Burning* (New York: Crown, 1960), pp. 103-104.
25. Trans. E. D. Ingraham (Philadelphia: 1819), pp. 42-43.
26. Soboul, p. 146.

27. Thucydides provides a remarkable account of this transformation on the instance of the revolution at Corcyra:

> "The meaning of words had no longer the same relation to things, but was changed by them as they thought proper. Reckless daring was held to be loyal courage; prudent delay was the excuse of a coward; moderation was the disguise of unmanly weakness; to know everything was to do nothing. Frantic energy was the true quality of a man. A conspirator who wanted to be safe was a recreant in disguise. The tie of party was stronger then the tie of blood, because a partisan was more ready to dare without asking why. The seal of good faith was not divine law, but fellowship in crime." (*The Peloponnesian Wars*, iii. 82)

Allen Grossman's Poem "The Department"

(Allen Grossman, *A Woman on the Bridge Over the Chicago River*. Copyright 1979 by Allen Grossman. Reprinted by permission of New Directions Publishing Corporation.)

                Siste , viator

Bereaved of mind by a weird truck,
Our fraternal philosopher
To whom a Spring snow was mortal
Winter — a wild driver in the best
Of cases, on the margins of
Communicability — exchanged a bad
Appointment in New Hampshire
For a grave in the Jewish Cemetery
In Waltham, Massachusetts. Across
The street from the University
And nine feet from Philip Rahv
He keeps his hours, perished
With little fame.

                His name was Boime.

"A very heavy business, Grossman"
He would have said,
If he had heard his own death going
The way it did.

               Immortality
Was our Summer debate. But in the snow's
Confusion blurring definitions
Darkened into mortal blows. Consider
The wit
Of circumstance which made that mind — alive
Unwriting, and naive —
Record its own demise on paper
As a flat brain wave.

               Who speaks for
Boime for whom
The University found just this much
Room?

   His subject was the violence
Of mind, and the duplicity of his kind.
There was a wound, he thought, deeper
Than doubt where love

          could enter, or
Look out —
Weary of the fateless civil compromise.
But that was not the wound of which he died.
He was a lousy driver who got caught.

An idle woman looked out on his burial
From her window
In the salmon colored house—

               a disharmonious fact
Between the cemetery and South Street —
Sitting on a bed.
Nothing can be said, except

               the passionate
Theorist is dead. In death he was
Unclear —

His aged father, like a gouged up root;
The bitter wife; the child of five
Who wondered how his dad would ever
Get out of that box alive;
The bearded bandits who cranked him down
Know as much as I do,

        or anyone.

He left his work unfinished. Whether
It was good or bad nobody knows —
It was not done.

        Somebody is digging
On your grave, dear Boime,
Who in that snowfall, when you died,
Was farther South than you,
Better employed.

        Your name is
Penciled in now on a tinny bracket
By a casual hand. A baby
Has been buried at your side.

        Since you
Died
It is the second Spring,
And nobody has set up your stone.

        God
God what a big
Thought, Boime, you carried into middle age —
Fat gladiator, treacherously caught
By a suffocating thin snow, chained
To a careening metal cage.

I am digging on your grave, like a starved
Dog burying a fact —

        If I say, "Boime, you
Were abstract,"

        then with a great sweet
Smile, even from among the dead,

Who don't know anything, he will reply,
Leaning a little toward the Summer

        under
His unbalanced cloudy load,
And with his lovely gesture of the hand,
"Grossman, you do not understand
The place of theory.

        Get off the road."

Revision of Section II Violence and Myth: A Study of Georges Sorel

1976-1977

Violence: From Morality to Morale

I

Violence can be understood, in Sorel's sense as the extinction of social action. It represents the extinction of relationship on *contact*. The warrior engages his enemy to terminate all future engagements with him. The long, complex history of person is gathered up at a point — and suddenly risked: "There where someone stood a moment ago, stands no one."

Violence in this sense differs decisively from the understanding of conflict or quarrel in Simmel's sense of *der Streit* which assumes that struggle conserves a socially constructive role even if it be increased in magnitude "to infinity."[1] But this allows the unwelcome consequence that no matter how devastating the conflict, the victims necessarily perish — as a functional effect — for their own social good.

Such unresolved implications of his principle surely taxed Simmel for at other points in the discussion, he recoils from them, however inconsistently, by arguing that only limited dispute is functional. Thus, as regards the level of abuse in intra-family conflict he says, "The strongest love can take the severest blows most easily." But he later says that if the conflict is *unlimited* "in the wholly irrational and turbulent case [where] the object of the conflict is suddenly eliminated [then] the whole movement, so to speak, swings into the void".[2] In other words, if the hostility turns violent and "aims at annihilation," it ceases to be socially descript. But this move evidently begs the question for it abandons the issue precisely when it becomes most serious.

II

Simmel says, by way of qualification, that violent death is the *border line* of conflict.[3] However, death is not a border but the absence of all borders. It is not another *space* we enter by crossing a line. Indeed it is not a line, because a line is defined as a division of two *known* areas. One cannot speak sensibly of a boundary — over which functions are performed — unless one knows both sides of it.

But why, we must ask, is one of the most acute of modern social thinkers driven to this error? Precisely, we believe, because he wants to construct an unproblematic sociology of conflict. He aspires to demonstrate, paradoxically, the social *functions* of a "relationship" whose consequences are — with any logical constraint on "explanation" — unknown.

III

The violent act is not, on Sorel's terms, significant for its consequences. The distinction between victory and defeat is transient. The warrior is bound, by his vocation, to suffer both. Odysseus knows he is "duty bound to stand unflinchingly and to *kill* or *die*." But fortune, not man, marks the distinction. The consequences of the battle are unknown to the participants at the outset, but that is not the consideration; for it is the willingness to face the unknown that constitutes, in the last analysis, the vocation of the warrior. What is significant, then is not the outcome of the engagement but the *willingness* of the combatants to confront the immediate possibility of death. This willingness includes deliberate martyrdom, as well as open combat. For Sorel, the martyr attacks *his enemy* by destroying *his own body*. It is, for that reason, no less heroic than the fight. Thus, the author wants to understand violence, not in terms of consequences, but in terms of will — as manifested in the risk of violent death.

According to the author, a man can achieve a state of moral sublimity only by facing the unchartered possibility, in the willing to risk, only when, in other words, he is ready to sacrifice his life. Thus Sorel not only asserts that a) morality cannot exist apart from the act of violence, but that b) readiness for violence induces moral sensibility.

Sorel holds it that Christianity cannot so much be understood by way of the Gospels but only through an appreciation of the martyrdoms that preceded and succeeded and the transcription of the teaching. The religious, as opposed to the philosophical significance of Socrates resides not in his discourse but in his unnatural (edifying) death. By the same token, one can understand *L'éthique vivant* of socialism not by reading Fourier, but by visualizing the general strike.

The sacred departs from the secular only, in other words, through the medium of violence.

The sense the *sacred* shares with *sacrifice* is not accidental. The sacred bond which is set apart is hallowed by the value one is willing to precipitately risk or sacrifice for its sake (but which in ordinary circumstances on prudently measures). It is altogether apt that the denouement of the *Réflexions* is entitled *La Moralité de la Violence*.

IV

Sorel's "transvaluation" appears less shocking, however, if one notes the special connotation he attaches to the term. Morality, according to Sorel, is the state of "epic-consciousness" won only on the field of honor. Only *battle* can evoke man's "noblest" and most "serious" instincts. Thus, moral sublimity is the condition of the hero at the moment of attack. It corresponds to the ecstatic abandonment of all the "civic virtues," worldly loves and material profits. Only *in battle* can one find true ascetics. Sorel goes so far as to deny the moral value of any religious conduct based on quotidian standards. This includes the monastic vocation of routine asceticism — the Benedictine rule of work and worship.

Thus we can under stand the morality of epic-consciousness by that term introduced in the exalted days of the French Revolution — morale.

V

Morale broadens the meaning of heroism. It cannot be restricted to the romantic, detached figure exalted, for instance, in Carlyle's work. For a movement that requires the recruitment of the great body of the working class, the supreme act of virtuosity has meaning only as a point of *inspiration* for the body of uncertain volunteers. The splendid deed of Achilles and Patroclus have significance only as they are reflected in the rejuvenated morale of their fellow Achaeans. Morale, then, is the irresistible conduction of epic-consciousness *through the ranks*, by exemplary acts of violence.

What is to be noted here is that however intimately connected the meanings of morale and morality — especially as both command the sense of "disinterestedness, self-forgetfulness and sacrifice" — it is necessary to mark the distinction. For clearly the self-sacrifice that is undertaken by regard to one's side, i.e., morale, but in the same act obliges the dehumanization and destruction of one's declared opponents constitutes *fractional altruism*. Morality is predicated, on the other hand, on the universalization of the principles of a decent life that categorically command, in the Kantian sense, the equal treatment of all persons — not simply the preferred fraction — as ends and not as dehumanized means.

Needless to say, it is not secondary question as to whether the bonds of association are confirmed, in individual crises of choice, by the morale of the fractional association or by the universal principles of morality that these associations are otherwise thought to embody.

VI

The discussion of morale should not be concluded without noting the separation Sorel makes between the heroic violence of combat and the "illicit" uses of violence within the institutional structure of civil society. These uses represent a *profanation of violence*, if violence is conceived as the pure and unadulterated expression of will, called up in the gallant moment of combat.

These profane uses of civil violence are:

1) Police or custodial force, and, on the other hand,
2) Criminal violence, (homicide and brigandage).

These forms of violent are "illicit", according to Sorel (after Proudhon), because they conceal and pervert its "pure" expression. The custodians of force, on the one hand, self-righteously conceal their *motives* in executing the victim. The morbid "triumphs" of capital punishment cloak, in fact, the obscene desires of a bourgeois public, *demoralized* by its fear of open and honorable combat. (If morale is the exalted virtue of the proletarian warriors, demoralization, characterized as the middle-class fear of violence, represents, in Sorel's code, the ultimate vice.) The prudent and timorous middle-class expresses its moral decadence in the vicarious torture of execution of an already defenseless captive.

The criminal, on the other hand, undertakes his act in secret, for the sake of winning sudden riches, and thus demonstrates, at the extreme, the "lunacy" of bourgeois aspiration.

Violence as "pure" will is thus profaned and adulterated in the first use by the perverse concealment of the *motives* governing the use of custodial force and in the second by the perfidious concealment of the act of violence. The police power conceals its *motives*, and the criminal hides his acts.

The profane violence committed within the interstices of the bourgeois order reveals the deep-going crisis of its way of life. It is the task of the anointed proletariat to purify the unsalvageable decadence of modern society, not by awaiting , but by initiating the apocalypse.

NOTES

1. *Conflict and the Web of Group-Affiliation*, trans. Kurt H. Wolff and Reinhard Bende (New York: The Free Press, 1964), p. 25.
2. Ibid., p. 112.
3. Ibid., p. 27.

SECOND REVISION   VIOLENCE AND MYTH: A STUDY OF GEORGES SOREL

THE INDIVISIBILITY OF MYTH AND VIOLENCE: ENTOPIA CONTRA UTOPIA

I

In bourgeois society, Sorel asserts, the measured relation between thought and action constitutes an essential *duplicity*. Thought begins with concealment and, following the inevitable delay of calculation, ends in deceptive action. Thus, thinking is identified with a private, i.e. hidden process. Men are careful not to think "out loud" for fear of exposing their mercenary intentions and, in public, candor is generally taken for a form of madness. If men are to successfully compete with, and exploit their fellows, they must not reveal their calculations; the mind must be treated as a vault. Taken from the standpoint of the *other*, actions appear as maneuvers that cannot be easily understood because they dissimulate, often as not, the hidden intent of the action.

The Cartesian dualism (mind-body) can be conceived as a philosophic elaboration of mercantile duplicity. The "other mind" problem is not a matter of logical inaccessibility but calculated of appearances. This duplicity is the prime target of our author's critique of bourgeois decadence.

II

The two strategic terms in Sorel's partisan dictionary are *violence* and *myth*. We have noticed that violence appears in Sorel's revolutionary drama as the extinction of secular action, and we shall see that myth correspondingly appears as the suspension of critical thought. But we would be mistaken if we conceived of myth and violence as another dualism. On the contrary, they comprise an inseparable unity. The union emerges precisely in the attempt to overcome the irreducible gap between thinking and acting. Myth and violence are joined at the extremity of secular like in a single aspiration; the abolition of prudential, i.e. duplicitous conduct. Insofar as Sorel's commentators have treated myth and violence as separate questions, they have missed a decisive point in his work.

III

Sorel agrees with Renan that myth does not enclose two elements, an inside (private thought) and an outside (public act). Mythic possession is rather an undivided state of heightened adoration, "free of reflection and all premeditated subtlety." Epic-consciousness is a state of intense and undivided thralldom. The mythic image, e.g. Delacroix's *Liberty Leading the People*, entirely fills the consciousness, and nothing else in the moment can exist apart from or beside it. The ego compresses all its energy on a single point, lives in it, loses itself in it. There is not duplicity in "epic-consciousness." It is a "one-possibility" thing.

In the modern world, where quotidian standards of utility have corrupted the rich sources of elementary enthusiasm, the only "pure" environment capable of "evoking images one can genuinely express without deception of self-deception" is the battlefield.

"Men," Sorel says, "who participate in great social movements always picture their coming action as a *battle* in which their cause is certain to triumph. These images, I propose to call myths." Thus, the mythic intuition and the battle situation are interdependent. If one tries to analyze them separately, one is led back to their underlying unity.

This unity is perhaps best expressed by Sorel's notion of the "general strike." One first inspection, the expression appears confused by the attachment of two unresolved meanings. He alternately labels it a myth, and then again, an *act* of corporate violence. The strike signifies, on the one hand, the "myth in which socialism is wholly comprised," and on the other, the "Napoleonic Battle" or simply the "course of social war." But this confusion disappears if one understands the general strike as a body of images capable of *evoking* the instinctive "sentiments of violence" otherwise dormant in the proletariat. One is freed from the world *symbolically* as one engages to destroy it *in fact*.

This symbolic freedom is effected, in the world of "pure duration" (Bergson); or, the "time out of time" of the "continuous present" (Eliade). The participants, in Sorel's case, enter this state through the medium of "sacred fury." Like the frenzied *Beserkirs*, the modern proletariat, possessed of the *élan révolutionnaire fébrile*, are carried over the barricades — out of this world.

IV

The myth considered in its relation to its subjects is properly called an image, and not a representation. In the subjective attitude of epic-consciousness, the warrior no longer accounts for the material obstacles in his path, nor does he record the objective passing of time. Indeed, as we have seen, there is no experience of time in the conventional (chronological) sense of the word. In the duration of the strike, images of struggles in the antique past fuse with the vision of the immediate combat. Sorel suggests that the aspect under which the combatants experience war corresponds to the "tone" set by the Homeric battles. Every heroic deed recapitulates, in the moment, the prehistoric ancestry of the deed.

Representation, on the other hand, are worked up through reflection, and are characteristically theoretic and objective. They denote, or ultimately refer to objects in space and dated events in time. These representations elaborate and attenuate spontaneous expression, and subdivide the "momentary deity" into graduated and measurable units of time. In Bergson's terms, the image *endures*, the representation succeeds.

When these representations are worked out systematically and propagated through the social structure, they are called *utopias*. Sorel does not differentiate these intellectual constructions as does Mannheim, for example. Utopian orientations, whether they defend the *status quo* (liberal democracy) or challenge it (the Saint-Simonians Universal Society, Fourier's "phalanstery," Marx's "classless society") are, in the most decisive respects, one and the same: they inhibit violent action.

V

The inhibitions of bourgeois liberalism operate through the borrower's ideal of "progress." Aside from its philosophical-historical significance, this ideal reduces to the proposition: riches may be gained on the morrow if present liabilities are sustained. Or, as Keynes was to later phrase it: "a case of jam tomorrow, and never jam today." In a world of credit, no one ever acts *entirely* in the present. Thus, the rational economy of time dissipates the motive force of all great deeds. The obsession with the calendar and the schedule which is essential to the systematic exploitation of human and material records enslaves the bourgeoisie, for they cannot escape time.

One the other hand, the Utopias that reject the *status quo* also abort spontaneous action, for their intellectual dreams appear too remote to inspire violence in the present. When people read Saint-Simon and Fourier, they don't act, they dream; but this dream is only the other side of that private world of mercenary calculation — on its day off. The romantic dreams of the philosophers enter the salons, but never the militant world of direct action. These isolated daydreams represent, at best, an innocuous respite from the intolerable duplicity of bourgeois conduct.

Thus "ideologies" and "utopias" come to the same thing: the eternal postponement of decisive, that is, violent, action.

The ideology of bourgeois "progress" inhibits direct action, for its paradisiacal tomorrow appears so *near*. The Utopia of the philosophers depresses revolutionary fervor, for their tomorrow is so utterly *remote*.

Not philosophy, but the myth alone can inspire the revolutionary act and "free" the proletariat from the mundane world. Then the mean-spirited and narrow-mindedness of ordinary thought and action is finally surmounted in the unmediated enthusiasm for the general strike.

VI

We have marked that the community of shared myth, e.g., the Socialist General strike or Napoleon's *Grande Armée*, cannot be identified with either Ideology or Utopia. Thus, whether or not the remote social ideals or war aims formed at the outset of the conflict are realized or whether the victors subsequently rationalizes the result of the process as inevitably predetermined, the social nexus induced by the mutual sacrifice in the duration of the struggle itself remains the unqualified form of community: the *Union Sacrée*.

VII

It is necessary to comprehend this critical social situation by an appropriate term. For this purpose, we shall introduce the expression entopia. By the utopian condition, we mean the intense but transient state of social solidarity induced by the precipitate danger mutually confronted by the participants here and now — in the literal sense of the term — in this place. It involves the immediate test of solidarity that transcends the mutually alienated self-interests of civil life and its established modes of thought and action by calling out in unequivocal demonstration of affiliation: the risk of life itself. On the other hand, this risk cannot be understood by reference to the passive calculation of a future society which depresses the direct engagement and hence suggests by the inaccessibility of its ratiocentric aspiration, Utopia (the ideal no-place).

VIII

To be sure, from the standpoint of the scrupulous socialist, the issue goes the other way around. The class war and revolutionary solidarity become values only insofar as they are oriented to the Utopian end of redistributing material goods on the basis of a universal and equal access (with the variance of need) to the means of production.

But if there is "no wealth without life," the most radical distribution of material produce (which may or may not be realized) but on the immediate reciprocal risk of life itself in the manifest presence of one's oath-bound associates.

The fatal risk, in other words, by infinitely discounting the future supersedes the question of material accumulation altogether — be it socialist or bourgeois — and releases for the duration, however short-lived, the heightened state of entopia.

IX

The tension between entopia and utopia is no small part of the problem of understanding the increasing multiplication and fractionation of terrorist fraternities whose conscripts to violence are indiscernibly caught between the affection and intimidation of the *camaraderie* of risk and the enthusiasm for the ideal of universal socialism.

The difficulty here is that there is no faultless procedure for discovering in particular cases the distinction between an act of "exalted submission" in confronting an otherwise "senseless" danger at the behest of his peers, and a purely disinterested act of sacrifice for a universal cause.

Moreover, it should be noted that if the intense solidarity of entopia frees the cohort to project the state forward as the incipient condition of a universal Utopia, there is a solidarity without division.

So accordingly, in disappointed retrospect, the veterans of the old revolutions or foreign wars recall the entopia as the "nostalgia for the front": "The only true socialism was the socialism of the trenches".[1]

NOTES

1 George Orwell described the confusion of Entopia with Utopia in his remarkable memoir of the Spanish Civil War, *Homage to Catalonia*. Orwell notices that the interposed solidarity of the front, like the ideal of socialism itself, transcends

the petty self-interest, opportunism and indulgence of civil life but he then goes on to confound the fractional solidarity of the front with the universal ethic of classless society:

> "In every country in the world, a huge tribe of party hacks and sleek little professors are busy 'proving' that socialism means no more than a planned state, capitalism with the grab-motive left intact. But fortunately there also exists a vision of socialism quite different from this. The thing that attracts ordinary men to Socialism and makes them willing to risk their skins for it, the 'mystique' of socialism, is the idea of equality; to the vast majority of people Socialism means a classless society or it means nothing at all. And it was here that those few months in the militia were valuable to me. For the Spanish militias, while they lasted, were a sort of microcosm of the classless society. In that community where no one was on the make, were there was a shortage of everything but no privilege and no boot licking, one got, perhaps, a crude forecast of what the opening stages of socialism might be like... Many of the normal motives of civilized life — snobbishness, money- grabbing, fear of the boss, etc. — had simply ceased to exist."

Orwell later notices that the heightened community of the front that he equates with an incipient classless society begins to break up as the "interest in the war" begins to wane. But he does not see that the deterioration of the fractional solidarity of comrades on both sides initially inspired by the risk of violent death operated independently of the doctrinal solidarity of universal society.

Epilogue for my Brother

by Albert Boime

Brother, Guide, Teacher, Friend

Under the best circumstances it is difficult to write about a person one has spent many years in close intimacy. When the person is a family member who died tragically it even more agonizing. Painful recollections and self-consciousness prevent thoughts from flowing and resist artful attempts to compose them. Yet, as I look back on my relationship with my brother Jerry I realize that it was primarily intellectual — that was both the great blessing and curse of it. We expressed inarticulate love for one another through the mutual exchange of our ideas, through the warmth we enkindled together from stoking our intellects. Except for occasional talk about our parents, we avoided discussing our personal lives and failed to support the other's emotional needs. This strikes me as the more regrettable — receiving a phone call from him was like a desert wanderer receiving a care package. I eagerly looked forward to the wonderful sound of his mellifluent voice, to selfishly grabbing the opportunity to test out my ideas on his keen intellect, and to hear his perspective on the latest news.

Jerry was the most intelligent human being I've ever known. I never realized fully the privilege of growing up with him, having his intelligent counsel close at hand. He read omnivorously and in depth, but he submitted everything he read and observed to a rigorous critical standard. He captured the irony in every text and real life situation, and would have made an ideal commentator on the O. J. Simpson trial. His philosophic turn of mind enabled him to place humdrum events and ideas, tossed out randomly, into a wide sociological, historical and political context. A chance discussion with him of the news in the daily newspaper evolved into a spirited romp through history and philosophical intricacy. His gift for taking the mundane fact or event and placing it into a broad perspective, linking it with a series of manifestations until it assumed a fresh character, was uncanny. It is difficult to measure the extraordinary nature of his conversation, the inspirational insights occurring at times like flashes at the moment of expression; analysis of political issues, of anything brought into focus to serve as a bill of fare to nourish those exhilarating intellectual feasts that were so much a part of every encounter with him. I recall our daily walks through Russell Square on the way to the British Museum Library in 1971. They seemed to me as enlightening as Bishop Berkeley's dialogues in the garden. He possessed an unusually speculative mind and the ability to theorize on as high a plane as the auditor could tolerate. He kept up a relentless probe of an idea until it could be exposed in all of its manifold political, philosophical and sociological potential. He was an elegant debater. Any colloquium presentation when he participated was a dazzling introduction to a rare, provocative mind. He always spoke extemporaneously, and I never listened to a speaker more inspiring or eloquent. He delighted in taking up the intricate threads of a complex subject and following them through their numerous implications, then culminating with an original insight that gave pause to his listener or opponent. He demonstrated his talent early in his academic career: the abundant medals and awards from his student participation on the debate team at Los Angeles City College testify to both his eloquence and to his prolonged thinking about the central issues of the day.

Nothing was playful about use of his intellectual energy — his capacity to convey the integrity, complexity and inexhaustibility of the intellectual pursuit was inseparable from his private quest for understanding. He rarely used his razor-like wit as a weapon to put others down or to exhibit himself. Rather he turned it on those in high places who abused their authority or made life miserable for others. His relentless pursuit of ideas was a way of clarifying the tenuous hold we have on reality. He pointed out the ideological contradictions of everyday life, breathing life into stultified academic discourse by challenging its most hallowed assumptions. He was the type of thinker who brought the best out of his auditors, leaving them feeling more intelligent than they thought they were. I never left off a conversation with Jerry without feeling exalted and empowered. He took seriously what anyone had to say, and made it sing with the wisdom of his high-toned feedback. No idea was stupid or could be; everything was a problem that needed to be scrutinized. He had this special gift of communication that he would not confine to the classroom and conference, but which he took with him onto the street. He was streetwise, and just plain wise. He talked in the same pitch to non-scholars as he did to scholars —inspiring listeners by nurturing their ideas with a meaningful context born of an urgent need to understand.

Epilogue for my Brother

This erudition was matched by an indefatigable enthusiasm to convey to anyone who was prepared to listen his immense store of original ideas and information. During his initial encounter with the faculty at Brandeis, his style was taken as "eccentric", even bizarre. Yet what they — and, later, their bewildered counterparts in the Department of Sociology at the University of New Hampshire — perceived as bizarre was simple the absence of cant and deadly academic socialization. It was his "naturalness" they could not tolerate in privileged academic discourse. That explains in large part why he endeared himself to "mavericks" like Eric Hoffer (whose *True Believer* crankiness appealed to Jerry) and Norman O. Brown. Jerry was uniquely naive in a mortified environment. He was always himself, whether expounding a difficult philosophical point like a Talmudic scholar in the Yeshiva or telling a "Jewish joke" after class.

Jerry's originality and unorthodox approach to academic subjects did not fit easily to the ostentation of academic institutions. He never completed his doctoral dissertation and he only published a few fragmentary papers. There was no doubt about his ability to express himself verbally. He dissected complex ideas with exceptional eloquence and lucidity, as his voluminous notes and the essays in this book demonstrate. He wrote beautifully, unhesitatingly, in brilliant original prose. Never glib although sometimes opaque, I always sense his mind grappling with a recalcitrant idea. I have guarded his illuminating corrections of my early manuscripts as precious testimony to his ability to examine with sharp critical insight material from every scholarly discipline. Yet he was forever wanting to reset the codes conventionally employed in the social sciences, and picking out the inadequacies and contradictions of a "scientific" social science. His own theoretical interest in violence defied the conventional categories of a political "science." His critiques of the specific content and epistemological assumptions of the social sciences had to be heard, however, since Jerry was extraordinary in his interdisciplinary gifts and in his mastery of the methodologies of sociology, psychology, political science, and history. Long before it became fashionable, he questioned the rigid disciplinary boundaries between the humanities, social sciences, art and literature. Consistent with his critique of the authority of hierarchical, bureaucratic decision-making bodies in an out of the university, he refused to play the academic game, to gain easy entrance through spinning out hurriedly written book reviews, obscure articles of slight importance, and, despite numerous requests from publishers, announcing the phantom book contract. He wanted to produce nothing less than a complete system of thought for understanding a fundamental aspect of modern society and he hesitated to churn this out in bits and pieces like a grinding mill. His intellectual integrity would never permit him to offer, as conclusive, ideas not fully established in his own mind. His tragic flaw was perhaps his ideality that forever prevented him from attaining a point of satisfaction in his work in progress. Every point had to be subjected to a careful dissection and probed to its profoundest depths in an endless spiral. Yet, without a Ph.D. and without publications he could not find a stable place in the academy, and thus Brandeis lost one of the most extraordinary and versatile minds of the epoch. Jerry's contradiction lay in his correct perception of the academy as a cross "between a carnival and an asylum" and his inevitable dependence on this madhouse for his livelihood.

Jerry had the highest recommendations from Hannah Arendt, Hans J. Morgenthau and Norman O. Brown; he was perhaps the most remarkable disciple they produced. Arendt placed him "among the most brilliant" students she had known and praised him for "the inventiveness of his thinking and the originality of his mind." Morgenthau's letter of recommendation to Brandeis noted that Jerry "has a profound, searching mind. He seeks out the most difficult problems — he wrote his Master's thesis on Kafka! — and deals with them in a profound and original manner. His intellectual honesty is exemplary." Brown wrote that the study of Sorel "was brilliant; original; verging into the profound; and like a fountain in the arid wilderness of the ordinary stuff." Trained at the University of Chicago when it was still profoundly affected by Robert Maynard Hutchins' "Great Books" tradition, Jerry took as his models the most gifted minds of the past and present. He felt the need to organize his theoretical insights into a classical framework as vast in scope and complexity as those of a Marx or Freud. This turned out to be a tragic flaw, for he never settled for less like the rest of us. He suffered no writer's block, but only the anxiety that his system would not be all-encompassing.

His research drew him into a fundamental reconsideration of the problem of violence. His formulations were overwhelmingly bound to his essence. He was keenly aware of being a Jew living in a world which perceived him as the "other," and this consciousness decisively shaped his insights and outlook. As a self-aware (as opposed to self-conscious) Jew, he saw the potential for warfare against Jewry that always lay slightly below the surface of civility's contrivances and etiquette. I never heard him say so, but it is possible that Jerry's work represented his way of trying to make sense of, or at least coming to terms with, the Holocaust. The Nazi concept of the *Herrenvolk* — a privileged and exclusionary group — bears a startling resemblance to Jerry's model of the "fraternal order." The positioning of the Jewish "other" in Nazi society may lay at the heart of my brother's construct.

At the same time, his original statement of the problem grows out of the coordination between his emergent new theory and a new and heightened consciousness of history in the early 1960s. It was motivated in large part by the cycle of domestic and foreign violence of the 1960s, and he tried to make sense of it by starting with a critique of the treatment of violence received in social theory and political philosophy from classical antiquity to the present. His work may now seem dated; yet if he had published his ideas in the early 1970s he would have been remembered as the theoretician of the 1960s. Ideas that he propounded then are now being amplified and reexamined within such illuminating gender studies as Susan Jeffords' *The Remasculinization of America: Gender and the Vietnam War* (1989), where the fraternal process in Vietnam actuality and representation is sensitively discussed. Jerry's topicality is also seen in the remarkable collection of his students' research papers dating from 1967 and 1968 which testify to the electrifying effect of his theory on their sensibility in that period. But the longer he held on to his ideas without publishing, the more they lost their direct historical link to the events that inspired them. Yet he remained acutely aware that there was not the slightest reason to exclude the possibility that ever fresh catastrophes were in the making for some social group, whether alone on in combinations with others, and while his theoretical framework remained valid as an explanation of one aspect of contemporary society, his conviction diminished in the face of his pessimism. Nevertheless, just before his untimely death he began to shift his analysis from emphasis on the structure of society conducing to violence to that of a possible organization of society that would allow for fraternal solidarity without developing the character of exclusivity that dominated it throughout history.

Ironically, it was in this period that Jerry was victimized by academia because he refused to engage in the very type of duplicity he analyzed in his theoretical formulation of violence. Brandeis, like many insecure smaller universities, had made "publication" rather than teaching the basis for tenure. As Jerry's colleague, Maurice Stein, has pointed out, had Socrates or Jesus been in the Sociology Department in 1976 they too would have been turned down for promotion! Nevertheless, to the end he was open and generous in making his ideas available to colleagues and students. His ideas have found their way into the writings of scholars stimulated by Jerry's thought but who never acknowledged him because the ideas were never published. His unusual competence in the fields of social psychology, political sociology, and social theory made him the type of classical scholar that is now a vanishing breed in the academy. His treatment at Brandeis, and subsequently at the University of New Hampshire, is more an indictment of the corporatism of university life than of Jerry's lack of official credentials.

This is movingly demonstrated in the "Tribute" written by a colleague for the February 1, 1977 issue of the Brandeis University newspaper, *The Justice*:

> You comfort us by what you have been; by having allowed us to share in your intellectual and personal genius, by sharing with us your gifted mind, your wisdom, your wit; always in abundance and excitement. You comfort us, Jerry, by the legacy you left with us, the fruit of a life lived in spiritual toil and commitment, a life of love and concern for the human fate. With that legacy you overcome the absurdity of your death, to live with us and remain our teacher.

I note that I have mainly addressed his intellectual abilities and have not touched upon the personal side of our relationship. Perhaps this is the way it should be in a book devoted to formal academic discourse. But I am also a brother and rival sibling with all that that implies. I still harbor deep-seated guilt feelings about my envy of his gifts and my failure to rush to his side when he most needed me. Our parents, whether unconsciously or not, played off one child against another, and each of us in turn knew what it was like to be a scapegoat. Jerry and I fought often as children (I remember my being the instigator most of the time), but in retrospect I realize we were acting out with each other the frustrations of being left alone much of the time. Somehow this got sublimated into first a contestation of ideas, and then — as Jerry took off with his studies — into a mutually shared excitement about ideas. I was not the ideal brother by any stretch of the imagination, but it was our intellectual bond that drew us together. We spoke endlessly on the telephone about our mutual projects, and in this way forged a loving collaboration that we never knew in our familial context. This also coincided with our mature insights into the personalities and relationship of our parents and greater sympathy for their skewed vision of life. My one really pained regret is that I never told him in life how much I loved him and that I owed to him the sense of fulfillment that I derive from scholarly work and hence the essence of my very existence.

Jerry's preoccupation with language paralleled the investigations of the deconstructionists emerging in the decade of the 1960s. The source of a message or text, the channel of transmission, and the medium of transmission all imply the infinite possibilities for mutating communication. As we describe the world, we make a selection from all the rhetorical possibilities we might use. In this way someone who is conveying information about something is continually aware of the possibility of conveying misinformation and even "disinformation." Thus an inevitable condition of self-consciousness is the ability to misrepresent the "facts," to knowingly or unknowingly deceive others. This exposes the other unique characteristic of human beings — that which philosophers have always awarded pride of place — their self-consciousness. This means knowing what one is doing, being able to articulate one's actions and the reason for carrying them out. Human self-consciousness is largely the ability to communicate, to ourselves and to others. Hence language is the key to self-consciousness. At the same time, the capacity to communicate through language involves the potential for misrepresentation. Every statement necessarily has its negation; every descriptive term belongs to a family of contraries. As structuralist thinkers have discovered, human thought is rooted in pairings of opposites like "up" and "down," "inside" and "outside."

The separation of language from reality and our capacity to manipulate it is intimately bound up with self-consciousness. The capacity to deceive, resulting from the ability to write and talk about things, is only a special instance of the more general capacity to break rules resulting from establishing rules. Linguistic structures are self-contained with their own set of rules, and any system of rules presupposes the straying from them — otherwise there would be no need of rules. Whenever a rhetorical structure imposes on us something enjoined by a rule, we are immediately cognizant at some level of the possibility (or even temptation) to contradict it.

Self-consciousness and the potential to deceive both arise from language. Not only are we able to deceive each other in principle, but we actually practice such deceit most of the time. We misrepresent to others the characteristics of objects in the world and we misrepresent our own mental and emotional states. Whenever we do this, the overt statement is negated silently to ourselves in the form of what Jerry called "counter-language." The salesman who says, "This car is a bargain at $3,000," is aware that he should be saying "But actually it's worth less than I'm asking for it." This would constitute his voiceless, counter-linguistic assertion. The salesman is not only falsifying the value of the car, he is also falsifying his own belief about the car, the belief expressed silently in counter-language. There are, of course, many obvious motives for such "functional" lies as this one. The deceiver always hopes to gain some advantage from the misrepresentation, whether it be economic, political, sexual or a combination of them all.

Not all counter-assertions are the simple negations of the overt assertions. For example, someone looking at an abstract painting may say "That's very interesting," while actually thinking "I don't understand that at all." The individual covers up an inability to respond by simulating a response. Another common example of this is laughing at a joke whose point we fail to get. Many of these misrepresentations of our attitudes and feelings are so standardized that they do not really deceive anyone and are in fact accepted in polite conversation. These misrepresentations exploit what Jerry called "mortified" language. Locutions such as "Good morning!" and "How are you?" are not actually taken as expressions of interest in the other person. Often when we say to someone "It's good to see you again," we use the phrase merely as a device to hide and deny the hostile and indifferent thoughts we might have about each other.

Jerry tried to answer the question "What is the reason for this type of duplicity?" by asking another question: "What would happen if all our thoughts and feelings were published on our foreheads?" The obvious answer is that there would be a continual state of war among all individuals. There could be no social structure based on the family if every sexual inclination was openly expressed; and if every hostile thought about the people we meet and know were stated, every encounter would become a duel. The process of continual censorship of emotions my brother described as "socialization."

It may be inferred from this situation that it is by a general agreement not to engage in violence, or in behavior which will lead to violence, that we refrain from expressing our feelings about each other. It is just such an agreement which Hobbes believed to have been made to avoid that state of war of every individual against every other which obtains in the state of nature. The desire for self-preservation makes life "nasty, brutish, and short," and the escape from this state is the organization of communities by means of a social contract.

This agreement sets up the civil order, a system of rules, laws, and conventions. In this system we agree to substitute rule-governed behavior for violent behavior to decide the outcome of conflicts of interests. Here compromise is mandatory. Instead of fighting over food, we resolve the question by bargaining. Instead of fighting for mates, we enter into marriage. In short, instead of settling a situation which involves conflict by killing off the competition, we settle it with contracts or promises. Inside the closed container of society, members are afforded security and a limited liability, for although they may compromise their beliefs, their lives are rarely endangered.

Now contracts and promises are textual and spoken devices whereby we guarantee our future conduct with certain words, usually in exchange for some consideration. Like all linguistic forms, they contain the inherent possibility of duplicity. In contrast to what you know about the corpse, your knowledge about the future actions of a person who has said "I promise" is very uncertain. Thus the more our relationships with each other are based on contracts and promises, the less we know about how we stand with them. To the extent that all our relations with others are based on what we learn of them through their linguistic utterances, we have to remain unsure about them. The prevalence of the mortified language in social situations signifies that the intentions (friendly or hostile) of all other people can never be known with certainty.

The unity of the civil order is gained through duplicity. The prevention of violence which occurs in the absence of civil order requires the substitution for that violence a linguistic and hence duplicitous approach to resolving conflict. For Jerry "the price of security is duplicity."

But if the price of security and safety is duplicity, the cost of that duplicity is radical insecurity about where we stand in relation to one another. Within this civil order we have created we bear the intolerable burden of never knowing our friends from our enemies. There is no way, within the community, that we can really demonstrate or prove a genuine affiliation with other people. The duplicitous exploitation of language is so endemic to the civil order that it is practically impossible under ordinary circumstances to convince someone that we are on his or her side. People who refuse to dissimulate their feelings are cast out of the civil order. This is the theme of Camus' *L'étranger*: the protagonist of this novel did not express the expected emotions about his mother's death and suffered ostracism. As long as I am misrepresenting my own feelings, as I must, I cannot believe that you will reveal yours, for I know that you know I cannot reveal mine. No matter what you say, I will not believe you except in the sense that I take your words as fairly reliable indicators of what your future actions in my behalf will be. The tragic consequence of this mutual suspicion is that each of us in modern society is always and forever alone. Jerry even went further and declared, "There has never been a human society."

But the need to know where we stand with others becomes very intense in moments of crisis or drastic social change. We need to find some way of ending the torturous doubt about this matter. This desperation induces us to seek and even create situations in which the affections and hatreds of others will be made manifest either in self-defense or in provocation, where we may demonstrate trust and love for others, and can see others demonstrating truth and love for us.

The extreme solution of the *civil* order to this problem is the field of battle or physical confrontation, a site where we must show (not just say) that we are willing to yield up the security for which the civil order was established and leave off the disposition to misrepresent our feelings. The concept of *proof* of affiliation consists in making explicit demonstration of that which cannot be demonstrated in language whatever our verbal promises of commitment. An instant is chosen to disclose the credibility of the claim and often assumes such familiar expressions as, "Will you stand up and be counted?" "Which side are you on?" "You are either for us or against us!" These are peak moments that entail grave threat, when we must risk our lives for each other.

At the crucial juncture, we are disposed to risk to avoid the isolation of civil distrust. The more danger one faces, the more one can be trusted, because one reveals by that predisposition a willing disregard for those civil values that attenuate affiliation through conventional misrepresentation. We can establish our comradeship only by putting our lives in danger for each other, and the strength of this bond between us will be all the stronger if there is a common enemy who provides the opportunity by their hostility. We prove that we are on the same side by designating some third party to be on the opposite side.

Jerry called the bond which then results between us the *fraternal* bond. It is in the fraternal order as opposed to the civil order that we know who our friends and enemies are. We establish the civil order to avoid the threat of violent death. But the civil order carries with it duplicity and the awful burden of suspicion. We retreat behind our masks. Only by establishing the fraternal order can we re-establish authentic contact with friends and enemies — only by going to war and restoring the threat of violent death we tried to avoid through civility. It is my willingness to risk my life on your behalf that demonstrates I am your friend, especially in contrast with our common enemy. As Jerry puts it: "The aversion to violent death conserves civility; the risk of violent death conserves fraternity."

The pressures acting on the disposition to risk are inextricably tied to the nature of language. Risk is a requirement to demonstrate affiliation despite civil constraint. The affiliation is no longer fulfilled by the verbal or written contract but through the oath; it is the oath that guarantees that your promises that act against self-interest are true. The oath brings a promise of unequivocal affection and companionship which is testable; it is a testament to the willingness to die on behalf of the other. Honor, not utility, is the mode of fraternal unity and exemplified the break with the condition of civil values.

The justification or interpretation of words spoken is itself an activity of speech. Therefore strictly speaking language — however ramified — cannot be deployed to assure its own expressions or serve as a judge in its own cause. We all wish to gain independence from language concerning critical issues. The civil order spends much time reassuring people by word of words that have already failed to assure them. Verbal proof of affiliation should lead to certainty in promise but does not. Civil uncertainty in political representation is so grave that rampant cynicism has become the mark of the sophisticate. Instead of ever getting an indubitable ground of assertion we get an infinite regress of motives and masks. We seem to be reappearing in the same scene over and over again.

The act of demonstrating affiliation requires a sacrifice that language cannot provide, substituting a hazard for that which was heretofore governed by prudence. We prove by an act that cannot be dissimulated that we are worthy of affiliation. The moment cannot be deferred. It is necessary to risk the condition that all duplicity is designed to serve. The problem is to recover the ground on which it is possible to demonstrate that our associates are not altogether governed by self-serving motives — the dilemma posed by civil society and its decision-making procedures. There can never be an unequivocal confidence in language because it is undermined by the indeterminacy of civil representation. Fraternity offers the prospect of restoring solidarity and confidence because the risk cannot be dissimulated.

As Egon Bittner has summed up Jerry's thought in a letter of recommendation:

> Setting out from a critique of the treatment of violence received in social theory and political philosophy since classical antiquity to our times, he has proposed a formulation of its significance as constitutive of fraternal affiliation, which he conceives as distinct from and alternative to the civil social order. The necessity and availability of fraternal affiliation is predicated on the presence of equivocation and duplicity in the civil order. Boime argues — and I believe originally and successfully — that the ideal of peace,

implicitly inherent in conventional theorizing, involves the traffic of compromises and conciliations that create as much distrust as trust. When questions about truth and good faith become unbearably urgent, a shift takes place from contractual understanding to fraternal solidarity; and this involves a shift in the nature of acceptable guarantees from promises and assumptions that are always potentially "two-faced," to pledges of fraternal loyalty the validity of which is demonstrable through acts involving the risk of death in situations of combat of various kinds.

In short, Jerry assumed that we have the need both for friendship and for proving our worth. Fraternity offers a resolution to both these drives, for by relinquishing one's life for another the individual proves at once honor and comradeship. Jerry held that the need to prove one's worth was more important than the cause per se. Confrontation, however, is couched in rationalizations such as morality or the holy war in order to make it more acceptable. In reality, the differences in ideologies are usually exaggerated to increase affiliation, for the commitment to a fraternity is actually independent of the ideology. (Here, if I interpret him correctly, I believe he was wrong: the urge to fraternity, like the will to live, may transcend ideologies, but the formation of a fraternity can only be ideologically motivated in a given time and articulated through ideology.)

Jerry often used the term "manhood" and "masculinity" in the process of clarifying the powerful tug of the fraternal order. He seemed to have conceived of the classical fraternity as mono-sexual and male. A woman would be a camp follower in a fraternity or would have the added pressure of having to prove her equality with the males. In this sense she too had to prove her "manhood," that is, take on the male characteristics of the fraternity. He did recognize the mono-sexual "sorority" — as in feminist cooperation — as sharing similar characteristics, but gave less credence to its existence. Nevertheless, his theory could easily be expanded to include exceptions he overlooked. Just as the idea of "fraternity" derives from the French Revolution, Jerry could have found in that same period examples of women sharing the same "fraternal" bonds in demonstrations and riots. Charlotte Corday's confrontation with Marat was predicated on her solidarity with the Girondins versus the Jacobins. Women in the French Commune of 1871 and, later, in the Resistance experienced the same unequivocal sense of affection as the males, and returning to the period of the 1960s, women in the Civil Rights and Student movements shared the exhilaration of companionship that the fraternity provided in the face of extreme danger.

One classic case study in which we may substitute "sorority" for fraternity is the experience of the suffrage movement, especially as it was played out by The Women's Social and Political Union (WSPU) in England between the years 1905-1914. The radical wing of the English suffrage movement waged guerrilla warfare against the reigning Liberal government, reviving in many ways some of the tactics of the older Chartist crusade. The militants directed their attack against members of the government and property in general; the parliamentary approach to winning suffrage was relegated to the background as they sought to demonstrate by their actions their firm commitment to feminist ideals. The WSPU exhibited some of the distinct traits of a "fraternal" organization, including monosexuality, candor, the willingness to confront danger, and the rejection of family that are found in the common instances of masculine fraternal orders described by Jerry.

The initial strategy of the radicals consisted of disrupting parliamentary meetings, and although this was safer than their later tactics, it was not without physical danger. They were often forcibly ejected from the hall and occasionally violently attacked by the party regulars. The crowds inside the halls were tame compared to those outside them, especially in the industrial north. There bands of hired thugs would chase the suffragettes, taunting them and physically assaulting them. One celebrated demonstration occurred on November 18, 1910, an event which has gone down in suffragette history as "Black Friday." Government inaction on the suffrage bill sparked the WSPU's massive march to the parliamentary building, where an inevitable confrontation occurred between suffragettes and police who were ordered to prevent them from entering Parliament Square. The solid phalanx of women pushed against the wall of police who could not halt the onward march. As the crowd began to taunt the humiliated police, the ranks broke and angry policemen began beating the women, bending back their arms, ripping their banners and clothing. Numerous women were injured, mostly by the police, but also by bystanders also dragged women off to side streets and assaulted them.

Confrontation and the threat of arrest inspired increased affiliation and in the words of one of the militants "inflamed those older in the fight. They inspired deeds of daring, and created eloquence wonderful to listen to — in fact, gaol-birds created gaol-birds." Another militant, bailed out by her husband, responded in anger to his action: "Men are not so single minded as women are: they are much given to talking about their deals, rather than working for them." The WSPU's exclusivism did not permit men to become members: men had become the enemy.

The fight for suffrage in the WSPU became an all-or-nothing-at-all commitment. One was either for the movement or against it. Family ties were broken, and other political and religious affiliations were downplayed. Membership in the WSPU felt like a religious experience in itself; new members had their lives transformed. One leader described the transformation as a

> revolution in itself. No home life, no one to say what we should do or not to do, no family ties, we were free and alone in a great brilliant city, scores of young women scarcely out their teens met together in a revolutionary movement, outlaws or breakers of laws, independent of everything, and everybody, fearless and self-confident.

This freedom from Victorian bourgeois conventions was countered with strict internal discipline. According to the same writer, "Nuns in a convent were not watched over and supervised more strictly than the members of the Militant Movement." New members had to be proven "true blue" before they were given militant materials to dispose as they so wished.

The movement was guided by Christobel Pankhurst, who in the movement's later days, went into exile in Paris, sending coded messages to her followers on the front lines in London. The extent to which discipline was enforced is illustrated by the expulsion from the Union of Christobel's own sister, Sylvia Pankhurst, who had been ruled guilty of making too close an alliance with the cause of the Irish and Labor. When she was expelled, she was told that "we want our women to take their instructions and march in step like an army."

Those who chose to toe the line found themselves isolated from the regular party structure, their families, and other women in the constitutional suffrage movements. This isolation, combined with the risk incurred by their acts, engendered in the movement "good, honest, healthy companionship. . . Our very isolation was our best protection, and made us loyally cling to every woman whose badge was a prison gate." Jerry's theory was perhaps best summed up by Sylvia Pankhurst who described a convention at Albert Hall in 1909:

> Throughout that great gathering there was a wonderful spirit of unity and not one woman there could wish in her heart, as so many millions have done, "if I had only been a man." No, they were rather like to pity those who were not women and so could not join in this great fight, for to-day it was the woman's battle. The time was gone when she must always play a minor part, applauding, ministering, comforting, performing useful functions if you will, incurring risks, too, and making sacrifices, but always being treated and always thinking of herself as a mere incident of the struggle outside the wide main stream of life. To-day this battle of theirs seemed to the women to be the greatest in the world, all other conflicts appeared minor to it.

As Annie Kenney recalled, "No companionship can ever surpass the companionship of the militants during the childhood and youth of the suffrage fight."

Ironically, it was the approach of World War I that put an end to the WSPU's militancy. Leaders began recruiting campaigns among males and organized women for munitions work. Those "who fought the fight for Woman's Freedom stood together until we saw our country free from foreign oppressors. Thus the fraternal structure of the WSPU was merged into the greater fraternity of a nation mobilizing for total war."

How far an unscrupulous government can exploit the need for fraternal union for wartime indoctrination in a complex society such as our own, is vividly seen in the propaganda of the Cold War. The process was perhaps best described by John Foster Dulles, Eisenhower's secretary of state: "In order to bring a nation to support the burdens of maintaining great military establishments, it is necessary to create an emotional state akin to war psychology. There must be the portrayal of external menace. This involves the development to a high degree of the nation-hero, nation-villain ideology and the arousing of the population to a sense of sacrifice. Once these exist, we have gone a long way on the path to war." More recently, we have seen how effectively President Bush managed to mobilize the nation for war against Iraq by condensing the idea of Iraq into the hated metaphor of Saddam Hussein. By creating an arch-villain, it was possible for the great majority of Americans to celebrate the slaughter of the Iraqi people as if they were cheering the home team at a football game. Rather than wave the school pennants, they bonded through the skeins of yellow ribbons.

Civil War and domestic insurrection also have their roots in the fraternal process. Social structures under threat become fraternized. Civil order breaks down and civil war results, for two fraternities in one domus cannot peacefully coexist. It becomes impossible for a single authoritarian figure mutually acceptable to both fraternities to maintain peace, for that would imply compromise which is incompatible with the ethos of the fraternal order. The "rebels" turn on their former sponsor by transgressing the civil boundaries. The result of the war will decide the correctness of the causes. Something like this occurred during the American Civil War. America had been split into the apologists and the abolitionists, each group totally convinced of their own morality and unwilling to allow the other to exist. Any move by the civil order to appease one of the fraternities would result only in the angering of the other, and therefore increasing its affiliation. Laws were no longer the only effective means for resolving the conflict. The rebel, in this case, the south, would become the criminal, and because it lost was forced to comply to the northern power. The "compromise" acceptable in 1850 was no longer tolerable in 1860, and bullets were substituted for ballots.

Like all inspired scholars, Jerry was a remarkably effective teacher and his students found their understanding of social processes transformed after working with him. His students, from whom I have drawn many of my examples, applied his theory to a wide range of social phenomena and expanded upon it by testing it out on a number of major historical and religious moments. For them it helped clarify otherwise inexplicable aspects of the American Civil War, the 1848 insurrections and the French Commune, and even could examine the process of risk-taking in the financial world as a subset of civil society in relation to the risk-taking in the fraternal society. A fascinating study on the samurai warrior code disclosed the parallel patterns of the Japanese Bushido ethic and the values of the fraternal association, while others discovered a fraternal structure within work organization and, at that time (1967), in the closeted world

Epilogue for my Brother 153

of gays. Struggling to find an alternative to the standard parochial approach of the period that treated homosexuality as an illness, perversion, or mental disorder, the student of homosexual association proposed that the structures of the contemporary heterosexual and gay worlds roughly approximated the civil and fraternal orders.

One of Jerry's students even went so far as to see in the New Testament account of St. Matthew an example of the theory. Jesus formed with his disciples a fraternal order in opposition to the civil order of the Roman-dominated Jewish society. When Jesus called his disciples, they left jobs and families for the sake of fraternal association with the Master. From the start of this affiliation Jesus informed them of his imminent death, and the need to yield up material existence to recover a higher unity of being: "For whosoever will save his life shall lose it: and whosoever will lose his life for my sake shall find it." Jesus decried the hypocrisy, the compromise, the duplicity of the civil order, and posited a mode of social organization which sought to surmount the civil order through self-sacrifice and denial. As he is quoted in St. John, XV, 13: "Greater love hath no man than this, that a man lay down his life for his friends."

The recent writings of René Girard have also clarified the relationship between the role of sacrifice — central to all religious organizations — and violence within the community. His book *Violence and the Sacred* attempts to show that sacrifice is a form of violence exercised against a single creature to unite a society and establish order within it. Ritual expressions of violence keeps it from running wild, directing a neutralizing violent impulses that would decimate the society when no external enemy is present. Historically, however, sacrificial victims comprehended prisoners of war, slaves, small children, handicapped persons and/or those deemed as the dregs of society. It is no coincidence that the unifying factor in this disparate group is that the victims stand either on the outside or on the margins of society, foreigners or enemies, servile, or those not full-fledged members in the society. Hence, the violence that is at the heart of the sacred is predicated on rallying a population around the ritual extermination of the "outsider" not fully integrated into the community.

Jerry's theory has also been complemented by the discoveries of the socio-biologists who argue that animal behavior follows a similar trajectory. An essential aspect of group territorialism is that members of a group unite when in hostile confrontation with another group that encroaches on its feeding territory. The united and the aggression from without are fundamental. Within groups there is often a pecking order and hostile relationships among members of individual groups. But these frictions dissolve during confrontation with another group. This temporary suspension of intra-member hostility is done by means of reassurance signals that indicate "I am a friend." This process, described by Tinbergen, strikingly resembles my brother's paradigm.

But one can open the newspaper any day and find examples, especially in a world in which terrorist action (state-sponsored as well as communal), skinheads, survivalists, gang-related activities, militia and vigilante groups have become commonplace. In 1978, a confessed "hit man" testified that in the underworld committing murder with a friend creates "a marriage between two people." He emphasized that in one case a murder had established a special bond between him and his accomplice. More recently, the experiences of Jonestown, Rajneeshpuram, the Mt. Carmel of the Branch Davidians, and the remarkable growth of the militia movement (linked with the Oklahoma City bombing) have demonstrated the cohesion of adversaries established around the threat of violence and the exclusivistic nature of their communities.

Not that Jerry's theory lacked flaws — flaws due to lack of time to work them out. Perhaps Jerry's theory's greatest fault is its lack of class analysis. Just before he died he had been working on this very problem, trying to integrate Marx's theory on class with his research. The various classes are quite conscious of their uniqueness with goals and interests opposed to the others. Whether in work, politics, or culture, an essential defining characteristic of each class is its antagonism to the others. Marx wrote of the bourgeoisie in the *German Ideology*: "The separate individuals form a class in so far as they have to carry on a common battle against another class: otherwise they are on hostile terms with each other as competitors."

Marx's prediction of a classless society in the wake of a proletarian revolution is a society without an enemy. Without the struggle of the classes, their antagonistic relationship disappears and with it the designation "class." Here is the key to Jerry's formulation of a resolution of the social dilemma in which human authenticity and solidarity and honesty may be achieved without having to provoke the exclusivistic character of the fraternal order. Perhaps Jerry's paradox of fraternal association and violence could be resolved through the capacity for *forgiveness*. Forgiveness is the actualization of *brotherhood*. We cannot exist without brotherhood and sisterhood, but forgiveness and tolerance create conditions for a fraternal alternative to the order based on honor and sealed by violence. Human solidarity of men and women predicated on the acceptance of difference holds out the brightest possibility of a stable and enduring society at peace with itself. The political response to Jerry's formulation in the coming decades will decisively determine the future of human society as it nears the end of the second millennium.

Sadly, present circumstances do not allow for an optimistic prognosis. Jerry would have seen his theory vindicated in the recent events following the collapse of state socialism and the re-Balkanization of Eastern Europe. Political expression there has backed into the future, with extreme nationalism, xenophobia, ethnic hatreds and anti-Semitism. The ministates in ex-Yugoslavia are at one another's throats in the name of transcendental unity. With the withering away of the threat of the paradigmatic external enemy, societies seem to be groping to find closer to home groups that they may construe as threatening and evil. This new nationalist, religious and ethnic fundamentalism has been labeled by Jacques Delors, former president of the European Commission, "ideologies of exclusion". This terminology agrees precisely with Jerry's characterization of the fraternal process.

INDEX

A

Arendt, Hannah *13, 28, 34*

B

Baldwin, James *4*
Bargain, The *99*
Bellum *83, 91*
Bergson, Henri Louis *61, 65-70, 76*
Bradley, Francis Herbert *15*
Brandeis University *79*
Brown, Norman O. *141-142*
Burke, Edmund *81, 94, 100-101, 105, 115-116, 119*

C

Camaraderie *137*
Cicero *87, 89, 103*
Civil order *82-119*
Civil society *81-119*
Commune of 1871 *73*
Confrontation with death *99*
Container convention *90, 93, 104, 109-118*

D

Domi et militiae *88, 91, 110*
Duel, the *99, 108, 119*
Duplicity *98, 116-119, 133*

E

Élan vital *86*

F

Fatal risk *86, 118*
Foucault, Michel *53*
Fourier, Charles *63, 70-71*
Fraternal
  community *98*
  order *97-102, 115-116*
  structure *99-100, 103*
Freud, Sigmund *85-86, 96, 106, 118*

G

Gandhi, Mohandas *100*

H

Heroic violence *64*
Hobbes, Thomas *83-118*

K

Kafka, Franz *4, 7–11, 11–48*

M

Mailer, Norman *3*
Malcolm X *1*
Mannheim, Karl *70*
Marx, Karl *61, 66-70*
Metamorphosis *7*
Militant oath *119*
Morgenthau, Hans J. *142*
Mortified language *145-146*

N

Nietzsche, Friedrich Wilhelm *85*
Non-violent *99-100*
Null society *93*

O

Organic fallacy *84*

P

Problem of violence in modern society 79, 85

R

Risk exchange *118*
Risk of violence *118-119*
Risks *118*
Rousseau, Jean Jacques *63, 72-73*

S

Saint-Simon, Claude Henri, Comte de *71*
Simmel, Georg *62, 105-106*
Social Contract *72*
Socialization *141, 145*
Sorel, Georges *57-74, 127-138*

T

Thucydides *98*

U

Unconditional sacrifice *118*
Utopia *61, 71*

V

Vietnam War *79*
Violatio *87, 91*
Violence and myth *59, 69*
Violence within *60*

W

Wittgenstein, Ludwig *56*